Influence with Eloquence

Influence with Eloquence

Classical Persuasion for Business Professionals

Gavin F. Hurley, PhD

BEP

BUSINESS EXPERT PRESS

Leader in applied, concise business books

Influence with Eloquence: Classical Persuasion for Business Professionals

Cover design by Cecilia Orth

Interior design by S4Carlisle Publishing Services, Chennai, India

First published in 2025 by
Business Expert Press, LLC
222 East 46th Street, New York, NY 10017
www.businessexpertpress.com

ISBN-13: 978-1-63742-852-8 (paperback)
ISBN-13: 978-1-63742-853-5 (e-book)

Business Expert Press Corporate Communication Collection

First edition: 2025

10 9 8 7 6 5 4 3 2 1

EU SAFETY REPRESENTATIVE
Mare Nostrum Group B.V.
Mauritskade 21D
1091 GC Amsterdam
The Netherlands
gpsr@mare-nostrum.co.uk

Description

Not Only Effective. Not Only Efficient. But Eloquent

For hundreds of years, great rulers, teachers, and thinkers have embraced the arts of eloquence—that is, stylishly persuasive communication. Yet, over the last century or so, we've largely forgotten about these arts. *Influence with Eloquence* revives these timeless traditions, connects them to the modern workplace, and shares practical takeaways to strengthen one's communication savvy.

The Old Is New Again

Spotlighting Ancient Greece and Roman wisdom from thinkers like Plato, Aristotle, Cicero, and Augustine, *Influence with Eloquence* outlines dimensions of powerful speaking and writing that many MBA programs overlook. The book gives you an all-access pass to the wellspring of classical strategies and tactics to enhance pitches, enliven documents, and enrich interactions. Offering more than simple turnkey tricks, *Influence with Eloquence* teaches rhetorical attitudes alongside their business applications, so you can become equipped to communicate in the workplace and marketplace with 360° vision and versatility.

Strategic Eloquence

An indispensable guide for leaders, managers, sales professionals, and workplace trainers, *Influence with Eloquence* uncovers the often-overlooked art of rhetorical communication. By embracing the rhetorical principles outlined in this book, you will energize audiences, cultivate deeper conversations, and forge enduring professional relationships. Pitches will become captivating narratives. E-mails will become instruments of influence. And job interviews will become performances of persuasion.

Influence with Eloquence will empower you to captivate others with every word you speak and write.

Gavin F. Hurley, PhD, is an associate professor of communication and literature at Ave Maria University, where he teaches rhetoric, writing, journalism, and business communication. He teaches for the communication, rhetoric, and writing MA program as well as the MBA program. Dr. Hurley can be found at https://gavinfhurley.com.

Contents

List of Figures

Preface

At an academic conference years ago, I ran into a colleague who asked me what I was teaching that semester. I told her that I was teaching a business communication course and some MBA courses.

She tilted her head. She seemed to think that was weird.

She said that she thought I was teaching classical liberal arts courses—Plato, Aristotle, Homer, that type of thing. I said that I was.

She tilted her head again.

I assured her that I bring the classical liberal arts into my business communication and MBA classes. She seemed genuinely surprised—and even a bit doubtful—as if it was utterly ridiculous to unite the classical tradition with the business world, as if it was an unresolvable paradox. Like a four-sided triangle. Or a married bachelor.

Rest assured, it's no paradox. And her resistance is not really her fault. It's typical of today's overspecialized professional landscape. These days, we've fallen into *either/or* ways of thinking, rather than *both/and* ways of thinking. So, from her perspective, I *either* had to teach business communication *or* classical rhetoric. And many institutions are guilty of this as well. At elite business schools, business communication specialists seldom teach classical wisdom. And at elite liberal arts schools, classical rhetoricians seldom teach business communication. People just assume that business communication and classical wisdom mix like water and oil.

But they *can* mix. Very much so.

Ultimately, typical *either/or* mindsets lack creativity. They stifle innovation. When we see things too specialized, we forget how things cooperate. We overlook *both/and* harmonies between disciplines, industries, and professions. We overlook the symphony of knowledge.

What am I getting at? In the spirit of *both/and*, the classical rhetorical tradition can indeed inform effective business communication. And not just a little bit, but 100 percent of it. The classical tradition has its fingerprints all over modern communication—from practical workplace e-mails to compelling product pitches.

The classical tradition brims with practical insights. And it provides us with a distinctive edge as business professionals. It orients us in the right direction. And its rhetorical principles can guide our communication decisions. These principles direct us toward palpable persuasion. They direct us toward sound ethics. They direct us toward charismatic warmth. In short, the classical tradition can transform us into eloquent professionals and leaders.

For too long has this practical wisdom been kept behind academy walls, hidden from executives, managers, and individual contributors. *Influence with Eloquence* brings this wisdom into the daylight. This book unlocks a treasury of classical knowledge. Once unlocked, we will use past knowledge to elevate our eloquence toward future success.

Enjoy.

Introduction

Name a song that moves you. Go ahead. Maybe one of your very favorite songs.

Have one?

Now, play the song. Close your eyes. Lose yourself in its melody. Let the music swirl around you. Let it warmly embrace you.

OK, play the song once more. During the second listen, listen analytically. This time, open your eyes. Think about the melody, the lyrics, the passion, the feeling, the message, the images, the rhythm, the tempos, the refrains, how it begins, and how it ends.

An appealing song that we feel in our bones is like an eloquent piece of writing. And a vibrant performance of that song, whether in a coffee house or a concert hall, is like the delivery of an eloquent speech. The song stirs our emotions, sparks our thinking, and connects us to the singer or composer. It unites us with the world outside of ourselves—and, ultimately, urges us to revisit. It persuades us to listen again, and again, and again.

Such rare compositions and performances are what we'll strive toward in this book. Eloquent speaking or writing is not merely *effective* as much as a wonderful song is merely effective. Nor is eloquence merely *persuasive*, again, as much as a wonderful song is merely persuasive. Nor is eloquence merely *influential*, as much as a wonderful song is merely influential.

Why? "Effective" simply recognizes a good speech by its effect. Did it get the job done? If so, then it is effective. "Persuasive" recognizes a good piece of writing when it simply convinces an audience to do something. Again, it seems only concerned with its effects. And "influential" means that an audience has simply undergone some change from the speech or writing. Big or small, good or bad.

Eloquence transcends these categories. It stands above these descriptors. Yet, at the same time, eloquence absorbs them all. It wraps them up and ties them with a silk bow. Eloquence is effective, persuasive, and influential. But like an artful song, eloquence also builds beauty and fans feelings. It pulsates with life. It is practical but poetic. It is rational but emotional. It is sophisticated but approachable.

And it is difficult to do well.

Its difficulty is why Roman rhetorician Marcus Tullius Cicero claims that good orators are so rare. Its difficulty is why audiences appreciate eloquent speakers or writers when they experience them. It's a rare treat to encounter an eloquent communicator. Eloquent speakers and writers comprise a small pool of people. And when we become part of that pool, we will seem that much larger than life. We will wield charisma: a seemingly superhuman and perceived spiritual quality. Much like a great song and performance, our communication will soar.

What Is Eloquence?

Eloquence offers the following broadband traits. These traits set it apart from mere effectiveness or persuasion. While each forthcoming chapter carefully outlines tactics of eloquence, the following rhetoricians' quotations can orient us in the right direction. These ancient rhetoricians offer six crucial traits of classical eloquence:

1. "In an [ideal] orator, the acuteness of the logicians, the wisdom of the philosophers, the language almost of poetry, the memory of lawyers, the voice of tragedians, the gesture almost of the best actors, is required. Nothing, therefore, is more rarely found among mankind than a consummate orator; for qualifications ... will not be praised in the orator, unless they are all combined in him in the highest possible excellence" (Marcus Antonius quoted in Cicero's *De Oratore* [1.28]).

   Interpretation: As eloquent communicators, we must wear multiple hats simultaneously. Eloquence involves the whole person, not just one set of skills. (These multiple dimensions are discussed throughout the book, specifically in Chapter 4.)

2. "… the foundation of eloquence, as of everything else, is wisdom" (Cicero from *Orator* [Sect. 70]).

   Interpretation: As eloquent communicators, we consult knowledge handed down to us throughout the years, decades, centuries, and millennia. This knowledge enriches our content and style. It enriches our eloquence.

3. "… the speeches I make on each occasion do not aim at gratification, but at what's best. They don't aim at what's most pleasant" (Socrates from Plato's *Gorgias* [521d6-e1]).

   Interpretation: As eloquent communicators, we must not merely flatter someone's mind or make people happy. Eloquence does more than compliment others. Eloquent communication is a beneficial craft. It pursues what is right and excellent.

4. "The very word 'eloquent' shows that he excels because of this one quality, that is, in the use of language, and that the other qualities are overshadowed by this" (Cicero from *Orator* [Sect. 61]).

   Interpretation: While wisdom and multiple skill sets are fundamental to eloquence, we should recognize that language drives the art of eloquence.

5. "The man of eloquence … is able to prove, to please and to sway or persuade. To prove is the first necessity, to please is charm, to sway is victory" (Cicero from *Orator* [Sect. 69]; later reiterated by Augustine in *De Doctrina Christiana* [4.74]).

   Interpretation: As eloquent communicators, we should aim to teach, move, and delight simultaneously. (This cooperation is fully discussed in Chapter 3.)

6. "In an oration, as in life, nothing is harder than to determine what is appropriate. ... let us call it *decorum* or propriety. [...] Moreover the orator must have an eye to propriety not only in thought but in language." [...] "This [propriety] depends on the subject under discussion, and on the character of both the speaker and the audience" (Cicero from *Orator* [Sect. 72]).

Interpretation: As eloquent communicators, we should embrace rhetorical communication in totality. To be effective, we must account for circumstance, appropriateness, audience, subject matter, and our own character. Eloquence requires a skilled juggling of these concerns. We should consider these elements in both content and style.

The Liberal Arts "Edge"

Our own learning is essential to eloquence. While language is important, eloquence offers more than linguistic style. The substance matters. It matters what we say or write. Cicero insists that the eloquent speaker or writer cannot solely rely on window dressing. We must *actually know* the content. He explains in *De Oratore*, "there can be no true merit in speaking, unless what is said is thoroughly understood by him who says it" (1.11). Style and substance work symbiotically. In other words, one hand washes the other. And this makes sense. After all, he claims, "no man can be eloquent on a subject that he does not understand"; and Cicero claims, "if he understands a subject ever so well, but is ignorant how to form and polish his speech, he cannot express himself eloquently even about what he does understand" (1.14). While we must know the tools of how to form and polish our communication, it's also crucial to know what we are talking or writing about. And according to Cicero, we shouldn't fake it.

The more extensive our learning, the better off we will be. According to Cicero's *De Oratore*, general content knowledge, *in addition to* specialized content knowledge, sets us up nicely for eloquent speech and writing. Cicero claims that we should certainly learn about how to be eloquent (as we are doing via this book), but we should also learn about other branches of useful knowledge (2.1). We cannot be eloquent orators and writers unless we have "attained the knowledge of everything important, and of all liberal arts." (1.6). Unless we recognize the subject matter of our speech or writing "beneath the surface," then our communication becomes "an empty and almost puerile flow of words." (1.6). So, it is good to know our profession through and through, but it will also benefit us to know some literature, philosophy, history, politics, geography, music, and so on.

While broad knowledge is great, we should embrace specific knowledge. As professionals ourselves, this point may seem pretty obvious; after all, specialization is paramount in today's workplace. Our expertise drives our professional value in the work-world. As a champion of the liberal arts, Cicero certainly appreciated the polymath thinker who knows about multiple subjects. Yet, at the same time, he recognized the value of expert knowledge in respect to a topic at hand. After all, eloquence fulfills the promise that a communicator can "discourse gracefully and copiously on whatever subject is proposed to him" (1.6), and that includes specific subject matters. For example, if we are conversing with someone about piloting a new home page interface for our company website, we should do more than meditate upon the human condition and cosmos; we should probably consider the specifics about web design, UX, ecommerce, and the history of the company's website.

Of course, we can specialize our knowledge too much, so we should walk a fine line. In his best-selling book *Range*, David Epstein makes an important distinction when discussing expertise and risk management. He notes that while specialization "minimizes the role of detours, breadth, and experimentation. It is attractive because it is a tidy prescription, low on uncertainty and high on efficiency." At first glance, expertise can drastically lower risk in a conversation. After all, the more expertise we have in a room of people, the more power we command. This power can be persuasive and magnetic. But conversely, expertise invites the higher risk of leaving people behind or sounding pretentious. So, we need to be careful to not alienate others when wielding expertise.

Anyone who works in academia, including myself, knows all about how expertise can alienate others. Unfortunately, academia brims with these sorts of missteps when communicating expertise. Professors often do this: when speaking to students and, even when speaking to one another. They constantly leave people behind in conversations and sound pretentious in doing so. It can be frustrating. It emerges from their expertise, but also a lack of flexibility.

That said, not all professors are guilty of this. While I worked at a particular university, a student once observed that Communication Department faculty were the only professors who were easy to talk to. We in the Communication Department did not see this as an attack on our expertise; instead, we wore it as a badge of honor. And the student's observation makes sense. After all, our discipline, the communication arts, studies the art of conversation, rhetoric, and putting audiences at ease. And as Aristotle tells us, the art of rhetoric can apply to any subject matter (1355b34-35). Therefore, eloquent speakers and writers should indeed be easy to talk to. Eloquent speakers and writers should know a bit about every discipline. They should also be curious to know more. Consequently, they can handle the messiness of communication: which includes unexpected circumstances and diverse audiences. They are comfortable when pivoting and adapting. They must duck and weave and be excited to do so. Naturally, such flexibility is much harder to do with only narrow expertise. It is much more difficult when knowing a lot about a little. Conversely, it is much easier to do when armed with a wide breadth of knowledge.

Let's imagine a hypothetical situation and assess our comfort level. Imagine that we had to attend a 3-hour gala of medical professionals, and we know nothing about medicine. Let's say that we work as directors of digital design systems for a payroll company. Could we charmingly hobnob with the medical professionals? Or would we silently stand around in our tuxedo or gown, holding a champagne flute, twiddling our thumbs, and wait for someone to discuss digital design systems? After all, we can only be eloquent if we have interesting content or perspectives to be eloquent about: interesting observations, interesting questions, and interesting knowledge. All the tips and tricks about how to speak can't save us if we lack content to speak about. As the adage goes, no matter how many attractive feathers we put on a turkey, it will never be a peacock. And eloquent conversationalists strive to become peacocks, not turkeys. So, let's do what we can to widen the breadth of knowledge and experience. It will make eloquence much easier.

Philosophy Is Eloquent (and Helps with Business Decisions)

The breadth of philosophical thinking, and philosophical wisdom, provides valuable perspectives to boost practical communication. In *Orator*, Cicero explains that philosophy acts as an essential element of eloquence. Like physical training can help actors perform on stage, philosophy helps orators discuss various subjects more eloquently (Sect. 14). Moreover, Cicero explains that philosophical training helps us think in an orderly fashion. Without philosophical perspectives, we would not be able to distinguish the parts, divisions, and categories of things, "nor separate truth from falsehood, nor recognize consequents, distinguish contradictories, or analyze ambiguities ..." (Sect. 16). Philosophical awareness fortifies savvy and knowledgeable speaking and writing. In *De Oratore*, Cicero also recognizes that philosophy helps us understand our audiences, specifically how and why they may think the way they do. And reading our audiences' motivations becomes essential when we look to prove, persuade, and please them, and nimbly respond to their reactions (1.51).

Philosophical principles fortify our practical skill sets. Philosophy's practicality is not a new concept. While it is often overlooked in today's modern age, thousands of years ago, ancient Stoic philosophers like Seneca, Epictetus, and Marcus Aurelius modeled practical philosophy. Seneca was a Stoic philosopher and statesman from the first century. Epictetus was a Stoic philosopher and a freed slave from the second century. Marcus Aurelius was a Stoic philosopher and Roman emperor from the second century. Like these practically minded philosophers from Rome and Greece, modern *New York Times* best-selling authors like Nassim Nicholas Taleb, Robert Greene, and Ryan Holiday also use philosophical principles to inform their practical advice to professional leaders and managers. And so can we.

Overall, the practical use of philosophical principles moves us outside of our egos, so we expand our perspectives and, accordingly, expand our eloquence. To use the language from Canadian philosopher Charles Taylor, philosophical perspectives open up our confident, generous, and humble "porous selves" and help us resist our self-interested and restricted "buffered selves." And, as charisma coach Olivia Cabane tells us throughout her 2012 book *The Charisma Myth*, genuinely open, generous, and confident mindsets naturally lead to more attractive charisma. In short, the openness of philosophical thinking helps people like us. Philosophical thinking helps charismatic communication and magnetism.

Philosophy directs us toward something large and meaningful. And it can be powerful to move audiences toward something similarly large and meaningful. For instance, although he is not a philosopher, Steve Jobs often gestured to greater meanings in his presentations. As *Harvard Business Review* (*HBR*) communication expert Carmine Gallo tells us, Jobs maintained a messianic presence and, through his pitches of Apple products, excited audiences toward making the world a better place.

Ultimately, it is the philosophical "why" that matters more than the material "what." In the spirit of the ancient tradition, the "why" matters as much as (or sometimes even more than) the "how" and the "what." The "why" opens up audiences toward larger meaning-making. And as consultant Simon Sinek points out in his 2009 book *Start with Why*, the "why" is a powerful position to place yourself. It can engage our passion for communication. In other words, it moves us beyond results to consider origins.

While Sinek's book is great, he was not the first to formally consider the "why." The ancients considered it long before him. Similar to Sinek, business leaders, such as Elon Musk, Peter Thiel and Jeff Bezos, depend on "first principle thinking." These business leaders have spoken about the benefits of beginning with foundational truths and thinking through strategies from their origins. Many people may consider "first principle thinking" to be a fresh concept. It is not. It began in the ancient world. They may also think that first principle thinking began in the hard sciences. It didn't. It began with philosophy. They may also think that this concept emerged out of American capitalism. It didn't. Much like the origins of science itself, it began in philosophy in the ancient world. It has been the guiding method of ancient and medieval philosophy. Much of the liberal arts' guiding operations are driven by the pursuit of first principles.

Let's trace some of these first principles according to Greek philosopher Aristotle. Such principles lay down a philosophical basis of eloquence.

Excellence, Communication, and Happiness

Upon moving to Florida in 2020, I met with a nurse for my yearly physical. She was competent, friendly, and professional. Like any nurse, she asked me a series of questions about my lifestyle. She asked me about how much I exercised. "I wish I could exercise more," I confessed. "Right now, I walk about 1 to 2 miles a day."

She exclaimed that my exercise is great.

When measuring my body weight, she wrote on the chart and said, "you're a few pounds over what you want to weigh." But then she immediately brightened up. "Don't worry about it," she said.

When she asked me how much alcohol I drank. I told her that I drink a few drinks a week but I'm trying to cut back. She waved it away as "not a problem." "You can have some drinks," she said.

I left the nurse strangely disheartened. She granted me freedoms, but the freedoms discouraged me.

I share this story because I see versions of my nurse's attitude all around us. Unlike ancient Greek and Roman culture, excellence seems to be less of an assumed priority. And we can see this new attitude throughout today's communication practices: the "good enough" attitude. The modern "good enough" attitude can stop growth in its tracks. While my nurse may claim that she endorsed moderation to help me become *healthier*, she also discouraged any motivation to become a version of the *healthiest*. The "good enough" approach seems like the path of least resistance. After all, even moderation needs to be recommended in moderation.

Unlike the modern drift toward mediocrity, the classical approach to communication does not embrace "good enough" attitudes. Instead, it seeks to transcend beyond the "OK." It hungers for more. It yearns for excellence. It does not promote "good enough" communication. Rather, it promotes eloquence.

How does this quest toward excellence work? Its groundwork can be traced to the ancient Greek idea of eudaimonia, which eventually connects us to eloquent communication. Eudaimonia acts as a primary goal or telos throughout classical ethics, including Aristotle's *Nicomachean Ethics*. Eudaimonia is the goal of performing well as a human being. Eudaimonia concerns human flourishing or living well toward the "good life." More specifically, Aristotle defines eudaimonia as the ongoing self-sustained contemplation of truth, which resists accidents and coincidences. Much like Carol Dweck's "growth mindset" from her often-quoted 2007 book *Mindset: The New Psychology of Success*, eudaimonia places us in control of our growth by ushering us in the right direction toward continual improvement. In this way, "good enough" is never good enough.

According to Aristotle, eudaimonia is "superior in excellence" and excites "its own proper pleasure" (1177b20-23). Aristotle's eudaimonia conforms the soul to reason. More specifically, he explains that life can be understood in terms of what we do ("activity") and our potential ("capacity") (1098a5-8). Each of the two dimensions inform hopeful approaches to mastering the communication arts. We can practice communication, but we can always do it better. That is the pursuit for excellence. Eloquence is a pursuit of excellence and cooperates with eudaimonia.

Our distinctive human advantage over other organisms is that we can practice higher-level reasoning. As Aristotle points out, we need to reason well if we are to become more excellent, and as a result, become happier as human beings. Since communication is a by-product of reason, to function well, *we need to communicate well, too*. In short, we are made to rationally speak and write to one another. This is what we are built to do. And it makes us happy.

This stuff can be pretty heady. But these connections are important to the "why" behind the ancient arts of rhetoric and eloquence. These classical principles offer a compass to steer us toward eloquence and keep us focused on becoming better. Like other ancient philosophers and rhetoricians, Aristotle is optimistic. In his *Metaphysics*, he claims that all human beings "naturally desire knowledge" (980a22). As a result, we all possess the capacity to build habits of reasoning toward eudaimonia. *While some of us may find it harder to build habits toward eudaimonia, we all have the potential to do it.* Therefore, if we act on our hunger for excellence, and act on our hunger for *eloquence*, we will become eloquent communicators in the workplace soon enough.

Mental Models/Habits of Mind

In his 2010 book *The Bed of Procrustes*, thinker Nassim Nicholas Taleb notes, "It is much less dangerous to think like a man of action than to act like a man of thought." In pursuing the excellence of eloquence, we'll be living dangerously. We'll train ourselves to be people of thought who are prepared for action so that we can communicate eloquently in the workplace. Active communication requires thought. And as Taleb points out, this action is dangerous but exciting. And as the business world teaches us, any worthwhile opportunities, if they are to be worthwhile, carry risk. And we require the courage to confront such risk in smart ways.

Eloquence involves risk because eloquence is fueled by decision making. Every workplace e-mail, utterance, sales pitch, or interview answer requires a multitude of micro and macro decisions. These decisions can be favorable or unfavorable. Each decision contributes to the overall favorability or unfavorability of the communication. And unlike mathematics, communication doesn't calculate clean answers and certitude. Communication, as an art, can only *approximate* success and that is where the risk lies.

Approximation fuels the arts. This includes the art of medicine. Aristotle points out that medicine's function makes people healthy but places people "as far as may be on the road to health" (1355b13). That said, it is still possible "to give excellent treatment even to those who can never enjoy sound health" (1355b14). Like medicine, eloquence works toward probability. Aristotle explains that the rhetorical arts move us "as near such success as the circumstances of each particular case allow" (1355b11). And every circumstance is different. We can move others toward persuasion or understanding without ever fully persuading or teaching them. And that is fine. That is the nature of the arts.

As an art, effectively eloquent communication is difficult to wield. But it is also exhilarating. After all, the possibilities and combinations are endless: varying dictions, differing arrangements, ranges of space between utterances, opposing inflections, metaphors, storytelling, gesturing, eye contact, font size, document headings, signature lines, this list goes on and on. And we must manage these decisions every time we speak and write and manage them thoughtfully.

So how do we do that? Aristotle explains that people practice effective communication "at random or through practice and from acquired habit" (1354a). Clearly, we don't want to rely on randomness. Instead, we can practice strategies and tactics of eloquence to build habits of eloquence.

As Plato notes in his *Gorgias* dialogue, eloquence is not merely a knack but a developed craft. And it does not solely feed the appetites like cosmetics or pastry baking, but it leads others to health like the craft of medicine. Eloquence is both helpful and healing.

Eloquence depends on habits that develop our identity, not merely our products. James Clear discusses this important identity development in his 2018 book *Atomic Habits*. Rather than merely chasing individual outcomes, habits concern systems and causes of outcomes. If we build proper habits, outcomes come naturally. If we only chase specific outcomes, such as eloquent speeches or eloquent documents, we must chase them every time we need to be eloquent. Instead, if we *become* eloquent speakers and writers, that is, develop habits of eloquence, we do not have to chase individual products because we will have naturally internalized the eloquent mindset. The eloquent products will naturally unfold from our rhetorical processes. In short, we should strive not to write better e-mails or deliver better speeches but to become better writers and more persuasive speakers, that is, to internalize habits of eloquence.

This book helps us develop these habits. This book helps us pay attention to particular decisions that lead to eloquent speech or writing. But like in any art, there are no turnkey solutions. Eloquence depends on optionality. While we want to aspire beyond "good enough" attitudes, "not losing" attitudes can initially frame our options. According to Richard Meadows' 2020 book *Optionality: How to Survive and Thrive in a Volatile World*, smart optionality begins with "identifying and capping the risks" that can damage our lives. When we recognize and handle risk, we position ourselves as "not losing." Ironically, Meadows celebrates not losing as a crucial win. He explains that "all you have to do is consistently not-lose, and you'll come out well ahead of the pack." To do so, he advises that we should "constrain our choices." Classical eloquence and principles shape a mental model to help us read the room and constrain our choices accordingly. For example, to effectively communicate to a room of 6-year-olds, we can refer to a recent Disney cartoon, and we should probably avoid elevated vocabulary and referencing Enlightenment-era scientists. If we are speaking to a room full of astrophysicists at a professional conference, we should probably avoid speaking about children's cartoons. With scientists, we can use elevated vocabulary and references to Isaac Newton.

So, it is important to constrain our choices so that we do not fail, but we should remember: The classical tradition demands excellence. We should raise our communication toward eloquence, rather than merely being "good enough." This balance of constraining allowances, both defensive and offensive, can fuel our rhetorical mindset and act as a mental model to navigate the world. Optionality is crucial to our rhetorical mindset. And Aristotle famously connects rhetoric to optionality. Throughout this book, we will constantly remind ourselves of Aristotle's definition of rhetoric. Aristotle defines rhetoric as "the faculty of observing in any given case the available means of persuasion" (1355b26-27). The art of eloquence offers an elevated and masterful use of that faculty. It involves recognizing what to do but also what *not* to do.

This book will help us understand the dimensions of that rhetorical faculty and cultivate a useful mental model. And while we should practice the art of eloquence in the world, we should also surround ourselves with eloquent influences and historical figures who speak and write well. As late antiquity rhetorician Augustine explains in *De Doctrina Christiana*, "Given a sharp and eager mind, eloquence is picked up more readily by those who read and listen to the words of the eloquent than by those who follow the rules of eloquence" (4.9). If we've ever learned a second or third language, we know how this works. Immersion becomes a powerful way to learn. If we want to know proficient Italian, we place ourselves in an environment where everyone is speaking Italian, say, Florence, Italy. Here the language begins to naturally seep into our habits of mind. Similarly, if we surround ourselves with eloquent influences, that is, listen to and read works from them, we will learn the language of eloquence more quickly and deeply.

Therefore, eloquent thinkers and writers are referenced throughout this book. They are the figures that we can surround ourselves with. Many of these figures are from antiquity, late antiquity, and even the Middle Ages. Since many of the classical thinkers and writers may not be familiar, let's look at a brief list of the classical (and classically minded) thinkers that will surround us on our journey.

Masters of Eloquence

Homer (700s BCE)

> Often considered the most influential storyteller in the West. He wrote the epic poems of *Iliad* and *The Odyssey* which are narrated stories about the Greek conquest of Troy and the aftermath.

Sophists (400–300s BCE)

> A Greek school of rhetoricians and philosophers who taught the aristocracy how to speak and argue persuasively. They were accused of teaching mere rhetoric without truth-seeking or sound philosophy. The Sophists include Gorgias, Prodicus, and Protagoras.

Plato (428–348/347 BCE)

> Ancient Greek philosopher. He wrote numerous philosophical dialogues that involve Socrates, another Greek philosopher and teacher of Plato. Plato wrote about the proper uses of rhetoric in his dialogues *Phaedrus* and *Gorgias*.

Isocrates (436 BCE–338 BCE)

> Ancient Greek statesman and rhetorician. While much of his material is lost (including a handbook on rhetoric), he was one of the best orators of his time. He was educated at the same schools as Plato.

Aristotle (384–322 BCE)

> Ancient Greek philosopher. Aristotle's important ideas survive via notes from his lectures which emerged in the Middle Ages. Among his numerous philosophical works: *Poetics* (a handbook on storytelling), *Rhetoric* (a handbook on communicating persuasively), and the *Nicomachean Ethics* (a handbook on ethics).

Cicero (106 BCE–43 BCE)

> Ancient Roman statesman, philosopher, and rhetorician. His *De Inventione*, *De Oratore*, and *Orator* inform the tradition of eloquent speaking and writing. *Rhetorica ad Herennium*, a handbook on rhetoric, is also important but may be misattributed to him. His speeches to the Roman senate are models of eloquent political speeches.

Horace (65–8 BCE)

   Ancient Roman poet and literary theorist. He wrote the influential *Ars Poetica*, which connected rhetoric with poetics.

Virgil (70–19 BCE)

   Ancient Roman poet. He wrote *Aeneid*, an epic poem about the founding of Rome that was influenced by Homer's Greek epic poems.

Quintilian (35–96 CE)

   Ancient Roman educator and rhetorician. He wrote the *Institutio Oratoria*, an important work on education and eloquence.

Augustine (354–430 CE)

   Early Christian philosopher and rhetorician influenced by Plato and Cicero. He wrote the *De Doctrina Christiana* which can be seen as a Christianized version of Cicero's theories on eloquence.

Boethius (480–524 CE)

   Early Christian philosopher who was influenced by the work of Plato. He was an important thinker who lived during late antiquity and ushered the ancient tradition into the Middle Ages.

Thomas Aquinas (1225–1274 CE)

   Christian philosopher and theologian who synthesized the thinking of Plato and Aristotle. He appreciated Cicero, Augustine, and Boethius. He is often considered the most important philosopher of the Middle Ages.

Bonaventure (1221–1274 CE)

   A systematic scholastic philosopher and theologian in the Middle Ages. Like other Scholastic philosophers in this era, he synthesized the thinking of Plato and Aristotle.

Dante Alighieri (1265–1321 CE)

   A Florentine poet and rhetorician who was heavily involved with politics. He wrote the *Divine Comedy* as well as works on rhetoric. He read (and was influenced by) Virgil, Homer, Cicero, Aristotle, Boethius, and other classical figures.

Looking Forward

This book differs from professional communication or classical rhetoric. While books such as Laura Brown's 2019 *The Only Business Writing Book You Ever Need*, Jay Sullivan's 2016 *Simply Said*, and Mary Munter and Lynn Hamilton's multiple editions of *Guide to Managerial Communication* are wonderful guidebooks, they coach readers on effectiveness, persuasion, and influence rather than eloquence. As such, *Influence with Eloquence* offers a more holistic approach. Accordingly, it offers a liberal arts approach where the "why" matters as much as the how and the what.

To that end, the next chapter, Chapter 1 continues discussing a rhetorical mindset that invites eloquent communication habits. It discusses the art of strategic communication in respect to the classical principles of excellence and rationality. Chapter 2 moves more fully into the tactical communication arts. It addresses the fundamental structure of liberal arts communication, specifically looking at the trivium, the interconnected arts of grammar, logic, and rhetoric. The chapter gestures to the classically influenced medieval tradition in connection to modern-day communication to highlight this dynamic. Chapter 3 then examines the drivers of our communication—that is, what our communication intends to do: to teach, delight, and move. This way, we know what desired effect we can have and how to combine them to craft eloquent speech and writing. Chapter 4 discusses the five dimensions or "canons" of eloquence: invention, arrangement, style, memory, and delivery. While some handbooks, including Aristotle's *Rhetoric* and Munter and Hamilton's *Guide to Managerial Communication*, are built around these five canons, we will only spend one chapter on them because they intersect elsewhere, as well. Chapter 5 discusses ethos, pathos, and logos: dimensions of persuasion and how they can be wielded to optimize the power of our prose and speech. Chapter 6 considers storytelling: a recently resurrected topic in corporate communication but indebted to the theory of poetics of Aristotle. In Chapter 7, we explore the "dialectic," a topic seldom discussed in professional communication handbooks. Since Aristotle mentions that rhetoric cooperates with dialectic, we consider how contrast and opposition elevates our eloquence. Chapter 8 considers how we can beautify our speaking and writing to delight and dazzle audiences. Finally,

Chapter 9 briefly discusses the eloquent lifestyle, that is, how to sustain habits of eloquence throughout our lives.

Throughout these chapters, we consult an array of classical rhetoricians from ancient Greece, such as Isocrates, Plato, and Aristotle. We consult rhetoricians from ancient Rome, such as Cicero and Quintilian. We consult ancient Greek and Roman storytellers and poets, such as Homer, Virgil, Horace, and Dante. And we occasionally consult classically influenced rhetoricians and philosophers from the Middle Ages, such as Augustine of Hippo, Thomas Aquinas, and Bonaventure, who integrated the classical thinking of Aristotle and Plato into their work. In sum, these thinkers outlined ethical and impactful eloquence. Accordingly, they were eloquent in how they spoke about them. Therefore, they have much to teach us.

In the modern side of things, we consult a range of thinkers on strategy (Robert Greene, Richard Rumelt), marketing (Seth Godin, Daniel H. Pink), influence (Robert Cialdini, Carmine Gallo), thinking (Daniel Kahneman), decision making (James Clear), storytelling (Robert McKee), charisma (Vanessa Van Edwards, Olivia Fox Cabane), and many others. Some of them have classical training (Robert McKee, Carmine Gallo, Robert Greene) and it clearly informs their perspectives, while others showcase valuable insights into the "how" and "what" of business communication.

Overall, *Influence with Eloquence* weaves past wisdom with the present professional context to help us become more eloquent communicators. This conversation between the past and the present helps awaken us to a fresh realization that eloquence is doable. It is not a skill solely for rulers, actors, and lawyers. It is a skill for anyone in the business world. But like any skill, it is built on particular attitudes. Let's first examine those attitudes in Chapter 1.

CHAPTER 1

Attitude Adjustment

Before we dive into rhetorical tactics of persuasion and eloquence, we should adjust our attitudes. In many ways, the ancient tradition thought more deeply about communication than we do today. And we can do the same. While some ancient rhetoricians, like Aristotle and Demetrius, immediately jump into definitions and practical connections in their work, others, like Cicero and Quintilian, spend time developing the mindset needed to implement the tactics. If we want to be influentially eloquent, and sustainably so, we should calibrate our attitudes toward eloquence, as suggested by Cicero and Quintilian. When we shift our perspective accordingly—and build those habits of mind—we can wield that "liberal arts edge" discussed in the previous chapter.

Rhetoric as Strategy

As Cicero explains in his *Orator*, eloquence requires rhetorical attitudes. And much of this book builds rhetorical attitudes to help us "influence with eloquence." But what is rhetoric? As previously mentioned, Aristotle defines rhetoric as "the faculty of observing in any given case the available means of persuasion" (1355b26-27). Centuries before Aristotle, Gorgias, a pre-Socratic Sophist, claimed that rhetoric bewitches or drugs its audience. In *Phaedrus*, Plato clarifies that good rhetoric should "lead the soul" toward truth (261a). Roman rhetorician Cicero defines it simply as "to speak in a manner adapted to persuade" (1.31). Later Roman rhetorician Quintilian defines rhetoric as "speaking well" and qualifies his claim with: "he cannot speak well unless he be a good man" (2.15.34).

Despite these straightforward definitions, "rhetoric" is far from a simple term. After all, there is a reason why we still choose to use the Greek word "rhetoric" instead of the English word "persuasion." Richard McKeon, a scholar of classical rhetoric and translator of Aristotle's works, argues that rhetoric shouldn't be defined as "persuasion." Rhetoric shouldn't be confused with the persuasive outcome. Instead, he emphasizes that rhetoric is a "power or faculty." As an art, it is defined "by its method, not its effects." Therefore, by thinking rhetorically—and artistically applying rhetorical strategy—we will naturally radiate eloquent communication. And to do that, we should closely examine and embrace the *process* rather than only the *product*.

When "rhetoric" and "strategy" are used together, people naturally think about manipulation: communicators who forward self-interested agendas. In his *Phaedrus* dialogue, Plato expresses a similar worry. In the last third of this dialogue, the character of Socrates explains that speakers should commit to truth-seeking. They should not merely appease crowds. Sadly, professionals have often ignored Plato's advice. In the twenty-first century, plenty of manipulation occurs throughout speeches and texts, especially through digital platforms. From broadband advertising campaigns to granular office politics, professionals can misuse rhetoric. Ignoring ethics, it drips with deceit. And, dangerously, it's shared online with lightning speed.

That said, manipulating others with rhetoric is not ethical. Moreover, its lack of ethicality is not particularly effective. As Plato and other classical thinkers suggest, manipulation is thin and fleeting while truth is confident and steadfast. By the nature of a statement being true, its rhetoric is persuasive. By its very nature, truthfulness is eloquent. How so? First, according to Aristotle's *Nicomachean Ethics*, when we are truthful, we socially conduct ourselves with love of truth and honesty in all circumstances (1127a24-25). Like Aristotle's other virtues, truthfulness is found by avoiding excess. It sits between the vice of habitual lying and the vice of being tactless or boastful. I think we can agree that lying is not persuasive (in a sustainable manner) and boastfulness is also not persuasive. Truthfulness avoids both extremes. So, it commands both confidence and eloquence. Furthermore, the pursuit of genuine truth is a shared enterprise. It is, ultimately, a shared pursuit of excellence. Truth-seeking is the shared fire that burns in our bellies, a shared human drive, and a shared dimension of humanity. All of us want to know answers about things. In the business world, this drive toward knowledge can help our companies grow. The shared pursuit of excellence stokes the fire of successful businesses and individual careers. And effective communication can fan those flames.

The pursuit of excellence within business communication relies on strategic thinking. As communicators, our goal aims not to flatter people's egos. After all, that is easy. Instead, we must seek to strategically construct bridges *between* our ego (as speaker or writer) and our listener's or reader's ego. A shared understanding of personhood becomes the golden thread of this connection, a shared connection to reality (outside of us) and truth (again, outside of us). This relationship is illustrated within Aristotle's *Rhetoric*:

Let's connect this Aristotelian relationship to the professional world. In his best-selling book *Principles*, Ray Dalio, who is CEO of Bridgewater Associates, one of the world's largest hedge fund management companies, shares a similar shared advantage. He describes this pursuit as an "idea meritocracy." He adopts this approach at Bridgewater. He does not lead the company as an autocracy (top-down), nor does he orchestrate a democracy in which everyone's vote is equal (bottom-up); rather, he establishes a meritocracy that encourages thoughtful disagreement and evaluates people's opinions in connection to their merits. Productive communication acts similarly. Pursuing excellence, both parties collaborate within a third space. It does not entertain naive relativism where everyone is right, or heavy-handed authoritarianism where only the top is right. Rather, it cooperatively pursues ideals in a principled fashion. After all, cooperation is not automatic. Cooperation requires energy and strategy to calibrate and sustain.

Cooperation between philosophy and practicality, or what can be called "applied philosophy," can be evoked through "strategy." When formalized and defined, "strategy" provides a useful way to understand

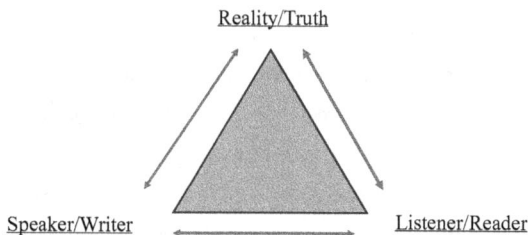

Reality/Truth

Speaker/Writer   Listener/Reader

Figure 1.1 Basic elements of communication

rhetorically minded communication. Strategy involves rationally mapping out decisions to forecast futures. Strategic action opposes impulsive action. It resists letting emotions cloud judgment. "Rhetoric as strategy" prioritizes rationality. As such, strategic short plays open up to beneficial long plays.

This rational understanding of strategy differs from the way it is popularly used. As some modern strategy gurus point out, strategy is an often-misused term. People often equate strategy to common grit, hard work, desiring success, or goal setting. While these facets get things done, we should consider strategy as a rational pursuit. Therefore, it is more deliberate and calculating. It seeks to smartly maneuver optionality toward a goal of excellence. Therefore, as communicators, we aim to smartly maneuver optionality toward our goal of eloquence.

How does strategic communication differ from nonstrategic communication? Frankly, nonstrategic communication acts as a sledgehammer that ignores situations and players involved. Nonstrategic communication hammers down cookie-cutter solutions. For example, if a presenter uses a script to pitch products, they are nonstrategic communicators. They do not strategically adjust their message toward audiences at the moment. According to them, one size fits all. While these nonstrategic communicators save time in reaching desired goals, it is at what cost? And are the goals sustainable? Furthermore, nonstrategic approaches undercut our ability to make decisions. They undercut our freedom to lean into advantages or lean away from pitfalls. They ignore Aristotle's definition of rhetoric: "the faculty of observing in any given case the available means of persuasion." That is to say, they disregard the "faculty of observing the available means of persuasion." They ignore adapting to "given cases."

On the other hand, if we are strategic, we sift through those "available means" toward optimal future solutions. Who benefits from the optimal future? Traditionally, as strategizers, we would choose options that best serve us and/or our interested parties. However, this advantage can serve selfish goals rather than pursuing excellence in the large. This egoism can be problematic. So, we need to tread carefully.

Let's look to Homer's ancient epic poem *Iliad* as an illustration. Rather than a handbook on rhetoric, this classical literature provides an allegory for proper and improper use of strategy. In the epic poem, Homer leads audiences through the tale of the Greeks fighting against the Trojans. The Greeks seek to capture the city of Troy. While half-god Greek warrior Achilles' rage leads him to fight fiercely, his rage also prolongs the battle which leads to more strife and death. Ironically, Achilles' rage also leads him to be stubborn and prideful. Consequently, Achilles sits out much of the story and watches his fellow Greeks be slaughtered without coming to their aid.

A main plot reversal occurs when Achilles recognizes the shared reality of what is right. His clouds of emotions begin to dissolve. He recognizes that the body of his Trojan archenemy Hector (who Achilles killed in battle) should not be desecrated despite being his enemy. In a rare moment of humility, he allows the Trojans to take back Hector's body for a proper burial. Here, Homer shows that the cooperation or shared humanity or acknowledgment of what is good and true is paramount. Rationality and edification break through the darkness of war and violence. That said, Homer's work is far from a children's story. It does not end with "everyone lives happily ever after as one big happy family." Instead, the war continues. While the epic recognizes the cooperative dimensions within the competition, it also recognizes that the competition between parties continues. This balance connects to effective communication. This space between cooperation and competition is where "rhetoric as strategy" operates. If we want to be eloquent speakers and writers, we need to strategically maneuver within that space of commonality and difference.

Another important warning about rhetoric as strategy can be gleaned from the Trojan War, specifically from Virgil's account of the same in his Roman epic story *Aeneid*. In this later account of the Trojan War, audiences hear more about how a large horse that is secretly filled with Greek soldiers was voluntarily accepted into the city of Troy, presumably as a gift from the Greeks. The plan was strategized by the Greek warrior Odysseus who strategized the Trojan horse scenario to deceive the Trojans into unknowingly letting Greek soldiers into Troy. Pretending that the Trojan horse was a genuine gift, a false agent of the Greeks named Sinon misleads the Trojans by verbally persuading them to bring the large wooden horse filled with Greeks inside their city.

How does this story connect to communication? In his 2007 book *The 33 Strategies of War*, Robert Greene argues that "communication is a kind of war, its field of battle the resistant and defensive minds of the people you want to influence. The goal is to advance, to penetrate their defenses and occupy their minds." Greene's "communication as war" offers one perspective into strategic speaking and writing. But is it the best option? Figuratively, the Trojan horse offers a representation of Greene's point. But the result is not optimal. As Virgil's epic poem illustrates, murder, death, and chaos unfold after the Trojans bring the horse into their city. Greek soldiers pour out of the horse and sack the city.

Hundreds of years later, in the later cantos of his poem *The Divine Comedy*, Dante places both Sinon and Odysseus in the Eighth Circle of Hell for deceptively speaking and strategizing during the Trojan War. The Greeks won the war; Troy fell because of the horse, but at what cost? Because of the dishonorable deceit, the relationship between parties is forever damaged. To put this in the business context, both sides cannot do business anymore.

In respect to modern communication, Dante's punishment of Sinon and Odysseus seems warranted. Unlike the Greeks and Trojans, we want to continue doing business with others, including competitors. We do not want to burn bridges. In this way, "winning" can be redefined. Effective communication is indeed about success, but in a way that "gains" another person's faith, attention, and respect so as to build relationships. Therefore, "winning" in this sense is noncompetitive. To "win" in a communication scenario helps listeners or readers—and allows them to win as well. Success results from establishing a win-win construction, and discovering the strongest cooperative advantage, not from establishing a win-lose construction. In other words, effective communication does not demand one-sidedness. Rather, it demands communion. It does not involve manipulating someone against their will. Communicative strategy rationally maneuvers toward a middle ground between selfishness and selflessness without ignoring each of their respective advantageous characteristics. Despite our differences and talents, each person needs to be essentially on equal footing *cooperate with* rather than to *fight against*. This simple attitude is central to building lasting relationships in business. And eloquent communication outwardly fosters that cooperative attitude.

Seeking "Omniscience"

Strategy does not applaud linear problem solving. Rather, strategy directly envisions branches of possibility (again, like Aristotle's "available means") and seeks how avenues of present decisions could potentially affect future outcomes. Strategic thinkers mentally map constellations of possibilities. Consequently, strategizers specifically seek omniscience, that is, all-knowingness, in respect to forecasting the future. Clearly, we can never actually become all knowing; however, an ideal, which is grounded by a sense of humility, keeps us yearning for a type of rational transcendence. This yearning can direct us toward favorable results.

In *The 33 Strategies of War*, Robert Greene explains this approach to strategic thinking. Although Robert Greene's book may seem like a playbook for politicians or military generals, the book provides valuable perspectives on strategic theory. Greene celebrates strategy not as limited avenues to immediately solve problems, but as intellectual maneuvers to foresee and even avoid conflict. Strategy works toward long-term goals while serving short-term goals in the process. To guide this movement, the art of strategy forecasts several potential actions: all depending on how situations can possibly unfold. It takes, what Greene calls, "presence of mind," to then nimbly enact the strategy in the present moment and guide particular outcomes in respect to specific circumstances.

How can this apply to communication? Rhetoric as strategy predicts the futures of communication scenarios, not to rely on one approach but to empower the communicator in the present: opening up a versatility of options so that the communicator can weigh and choose particular actions. Ultimately, for our purposes, strategic communication involves mapping out the probabilities about what resistant or nonresistant audiences may be thinking and feeling. Communication strategists rationally predict audiences' reactions and act on these predictions with enough flexibility to shift. In many ways, communication strategists predict audiences' desires and then work with those desires so that audiences appreciate the speakers or writers and their content. As a result, audiences appropriately understand, and may even adopt, the writers' or speaker's ideas.

For example, imagine that you are an entrepreneur seeking funding. You are pitching an idea to a team of investors in a Denver office. In the funding pitch, you first recognize the skeptical look in the eyes of the investors: social smiles (rather than genuine smiles) and shifting eyes (rather than sustained eye contact). You notice their skepticism when you first shake their hands. Based on this information, you introduce yourself with a personal confession about it being your first time visiting Colorado as a New Yorker. You make a few quick good-humored observations about the differences between the regions. Since you've researched your audience, you know that two of the potential investors also live in New York. You figure that this candor and connection will help lessen the tension. It seems to work. The investors from New York smile and laugh. Your subtle humor and candor showcase your comfort and confidence. You also sneak into your introduction that, despite being a New Yorker, you have rock climbing experience and appreciate the rock-climbing opportunities in Colorado. Finally, you fire up your slide deck. Your first slide displays a picture of the Rocky Mountains. You narrate a hypothetical scenario where the investors imagine climbing the mountain. You paint a word picture and tell an action-driven narrative about journeying up the mountain, which is something interesting and unique that speaks to your rock-climbing experience, and, of course, connects to the Colorado region. You then crucially connect that rock-climbing narration to the product you are pitching. You then move to the product's details.

This brief example showcases rhetoric as strategy. You first identify the audience as skeptical and resistant, then you shift to get them to like you. If you didn't take time to warm them up, the pitch would likely fail—or perhaps worse, be seen as mediocre. You are relatively sure of that outcome. That failure would be a future outcome based on particular decisions. You didn't like that possible outcome, so you strategically reshaped the introduction of the pitch. If the investors were more receptive from the beginning, you could probably jump directly into the product discussion. But instead, you needed to build rapport, cultivate warmth, build trust, and open their imaginations. Only after you did that could you introduce the product. In sum, you rationally imagined and forecasted results for multiple combinations and chose the best "available means."

Rhetoric as strategy depends upon forecasting. In *The Art of Strategy*, a book on game theory, Dixit and Nalebuff explain specific ways to forecast future possibilities. As strategists, they advise us to "look forward but reason backward" whereby we calculate certain outcomes and evaluate the advantages for ourselves and other parties. We reason backward to ourselves by calculating how we reach those favorable outcomes. For example, think about the game of chess. A chess player thinks backward from capturing the king toward the steps that lead toward that outcome. Simple games with several possible outcomes are not too difficult to map out, even for beginning strategists. However, complex games may require a table or visual "game tree" diagram to keep track of multiple outcome evaluations.

At first glance, rhetoric as strategy does not seem like a manageable game, even when using technological advantages. Rhetorical communication offers a game with infinite choices. Rhetorical choices connect to micro-level effects, each of which build toward palpable impressions on audiences. Every paragraph, every indentation, every word, every syllable, every silence, and every bit of white space on a page are choices made by the communicator. These choices have outcomes. They accumulate. Among the crucial implications, these choices affect how (and if) a reader or listener understands the message, and how (and if) they trust the communicator. Therefore, these rhetorical choices require risk analysis and strategy. However, we cannot build game trees for every utterance we say; we cannot construct option tables for every sentence we write. It would be a herculean task. Consequently, in life, often we neglect these communication choices. As such, we can throw away our chances to be riveting speakers or writers. We waste our opportunities. We settle for boilerplate conventions, or bland artificial intelligence (AI) writing, that may be halfheartedly effective but not particularly persuasive. Or even worse, sometimes we settle for mediocrity or bad communication merely because thinking about communication takes too much effort.

When facing such overwhelming complexity, it is useful to have instrumental guiding principles to help manage these choices—and develop habits of eloquence. Such principles can help us prioritize particular cognitive workflow regarding communication choices. An organizing principle can help us become more efficient and more effective communicators.

A fundamental principle can provide the instrumental means to attack the daunting task of communication.

Strategic Pragmatism

In his 2011 best-selling book *Good Strategy/Bad Strategy*, strategic consultant Richard Rumelt expresses his frustration for the misuse of the word "strategy." He explains that often the word is used to denote "big-picture direction" separated from any actual implementation. This separation reveals a notable problem with the word "strategy" in the professional sphere. Executives often have trouble, not with thoughtful strategic plans but with the execution of strategic plans. As a result, strategy becomes conflated with desire or goal setting, which is an important aspect of execution, but it is not the same as being fully strategic. Expressing a desire for a goal doesn't get anything done. Merely *wanting* to be a better communicator does not actually apply strategy of communication.

To explain "good strategy," Rumelt breaks it down into a logical scaffold that he labels the "kernel of strategy." His straightforward blueprint involves a three-part sequence: (1) a diagnosis, (2) a guiding policy, and (3) a set of cohesive actions. Although Rumelt generally demonstrates his blueprint of "good strategy" within high-stakes business deals and political decision making, everyday workplace communication can consult his blueprint as well.

In pursuit of actionable strategy, Rumelt explains that "good strategy" first begins with an initial diagnosis to establish a "domain of action" and seek "leverage over outcomes." The diagnosis looks to simplify a complex reality to discern the crux of the challenge. In rhetorical terms, this is called the "exigence." It sparks the reason to communicate. After all, without a problem or deficiency, why say or write anything? The exigence helps focus the rhetorical purposes and decision making.

Naturally, we can lose focus on exigencies throughout any given day—and it can undercut our communication opportunities. For example, let's imagine that an entrepreneur, Kelly, looks to persuade a 79-year-old investor, Cheryl, a woman who doesn't know much about the latest Internet trends, to invest money in her online commerce business venture. The two professionals meet at a local coffee shop to discuss the vision.

To demonstrate her knowledge about website development, Kelly weaves Internet jargon and technical terms into the conversation when speaking to the potential investor. The older Cheryl becomes confused about what particular words mean. Cheryl soon becomes frustrated. After all, the entrepreneur seems capable and passionate, but the investor does not clearly understand the words that Kelly uses to describe the business. As a result, Cheryl does not invest.

As this hypothetical scenario illustrates, Kelly ignores the exigence or need that fuels the communication situation. The exigence was that she needed funding. Cheryl could have solved this need. However, Kelly became concerned with showcasing her expertise, which corresponded to a different exigence (regarding knowledgeability). In the book *The Art of Strategy*, Dixit and Nalebuff similarly note that strategic thinking involves various moving parts. It requires knowing perspectives and interactions of the other players of the "game," including the silent ones. Therefore, when thinking strategically about communication, we need to be perceptive when communicating and when planning our communication. We should keep an eye on solving our diagnoses. We need to think rhetorically toward our primary aims, not imaginary ones we may construct in our heads.

Rumelt's second step of "good strategy" establishes guiding policy for handling the particular challenges or exigencies. He explains that "good strategy" emerges from a specific argument. The argument justifies a guiding policy that informs the actions that remedy the diagnosis. If strong and sober reasons support a particular way to solve a diagnosis, then that policy can be justifiably applied. A justified policy helps decision-making operations maybe not in every life situation, but rather, when solving particular challenges. This focus is why the initial strategic diagnosis is so important. It keeps the policy focused on the goals of our communication.

Policy creation can organize the cognitive workflow in our minds, specifically the complex decision making involved with communication. A policy informed by a unified argument helps pump rationality into the decision-making process. Or at the very least, a policy ensures the reasonability of intellectually supported future actions. It helps players in the communication game remain grounded, stable, and consistent. Of course, the quality of the reasoning matters. The reasoning can be strong, that is, informed by a diagnosis and driven toward action. Or it can be weak, that is, impulsive and impatient. The former leads to influential eloquence; the latter, not so much.

For example, I played soccer for over 18 years under a variety of coaches. In a youth soccer league, one coach promoted that the ball should go forward toward the opposing goal every time we possessed the ball. He told us to kick the soccer ball toward the opposing side of the field, ignoring the possibility that we would lose possession of the ball. From the sideline, he would yell sage advice: "Boot it!" Which is to say, he wanted us to kick the ball really far down the field. The farther that one of our players "booted" the ball, the more he would clap and encourage us.

While my coach was a good guy, his strategy was not well-thought out. He assumed that the closer the ball is to the opposing team's goal, the closer the ball is to being *in* the goal. A smarter, more complex strategy focuses on controlling the ball and moving horizontally, and even backward, to move forward. In this way, the team patiently finds opportunities to advance to the opposing net, based on vulnerabilities or weaknesses in the opposing team's defensive armor. Professional soccer teams adopt this more sophisticated horizontal-mixed-with-forward strategy. As professionals ourselves, we also want to adopt such a strategy. Much like an amateur soccer team, going only forward with our communication will look and sound amateur and lack eloquence. Instead, we want to be patient. Like professional soccer teams, we can move sideways and even backward to move forward.

Patience, Process, and Product

Actions are clearly important. Nevertheless, sometimes we rush toward action without thinking about why we enact them. Like my youth soccer coach's approach, sometimes we think impatiently—and we kick the ball down the field as hard as we can. We sprint toward the product (persuasion), unconcerned with the process (our "faculty of observing the means of persuasion in a given case"). Often, this zealousness can get us into trouble, especially if we seek to build sustainable professional relationships through our communication. Consequently, to be truly eloquent, we need to understand and ultimately develop patient mindsets.

There are several types of patience in the ancient Greek world. The word "patient" comes from the Latin root for "suffering." Unlike the modern understanding of patience as passive waiting, ancient patience was active, virtuous, and courageous. In the ancient times, there were at least two types of patience: *makrothumia* and *hypomonē*. *Makrothumia* concerns patience when around people—so that we do not become upset if the circumstances do not require us to do so. This patience can also be called being good-tempered. According to Aristotle, the good-tempered person "tends to be unperturbed and not to be led by passion"; furthermore, the good-tempered person "is thought to err more rather in the direction of deficiency;" and "is ready to pardon, not eager to extract penalty" (1126a1-2). People who practice *makrothumia* are attuned to the circumstances and behave conservatively to other people rather than rashly. The second type of patience, *hypomonē*, is less focused on people but concerns steadily moving forward in one's life in general: resolutely continuing toward a goal despite any obstacles. Both types of patience are fueled by fortitude: to persevere through trials and pain.

Like the ancient concepts of *makrothumia* and *hypomonē*, eloquent speaking and writing is patient. It involves steadfastness and perseverance. Its process is patient. Its product is patient. To engineer an effective speech, presentation, or even e-mail takes time. Its contrary, impatience, leads to the opposite of eloquence, which may not result in altogether failure, but often "good enough" mediocrity and blandness. For example, while artificial intelligence can be used as a tool, some people use artificial intelligence to write documents in full: an approach driven by impatience, and by classical standards, a lack of fortitude. Instead of wrestling with lengthier processes, which can lead to eloquent products, impatient communicators may farm out their process to a set of algorithms. The result: bland writing that lacks eloquence. Why? Because it lacks rhetorical effort and humanity. Writers who rely completely on generative AI are not *in* the writing. And the lack of intimacy and sincerity can be felt by the audience: consciously or subconsciously. The writing may be "effective" in conveying information, but it will not be eloquent in conveying wisdom. It does not create memorable experiences for readers.

So overall, we can embrace patient processes and tackle them with fortitude. If we seek to e-mail to an important client, we can draft it today, revisit it tomorrow, revise it with fresh eyes, and send it then. If we have a sales pitch next month, we can begin chipping away at it today. We don't have to wait until the last minute. When we embrace our process, we patiently work on our compositions over longer periods of time. It can help us make sound rhetorical decisions, incorporate them more mindfully into our products, and foster richer relationships with our audiences.

Audience and Expectations

A final essential attitude about eloquence concerns audience and circumstance. Both elements fuel rhetorical communication. While some dimensions of eloquence are shared across audiences and circumstances, others differ depending on who we speak and write to. The better that we know our audience, the better our chances of connecting to them. Different audiences will find different types of writing and speaking to be eloquent. For instance, in a famous early scene in the 1987 film *Wall Street*, novice broker Bud Fox lands a meeting with millionaire businessman and corporate raider Gordon Gekko. Bud Fox sheepishly sits in Gekko's extravagant office as Gekko passionately answers important phone calls. On these calls, Gekko speaks almost exclusively in metaphors and similes, including "this turkey is totally brain dead," "if this guy owned a funeral parlor, no one would die," and "Christmas is over, business is business." Now Gekko's figurative language corresponds to aggressive takeover plays. So, the language may not be seen as beautiful in the traditional sense, but some viewers of the film may see Gekko's speaking to be eloquent in its own way. Perhaps, a veteran businessman, who worked in highly competitive 1980s New York City, may find this scene eloquent. Someone younger in today's workforce may find the scene off-putting, not eloquent, or not even understandable. In short, eloquence should not be seen as totally relativistic, but relativity plays a role. We should account for how our audience sees the world.

Along those lines, we should consider, "Will my specific audience understand what I am saying or writing?" and "Will they be moved by what I am saying and writing." After all, a boring speaker's TED talk may not be eloquent to a viewer. Now, the speaker himself may not be *bad* at speaking; he may be OK. He may never stumble over his words;

he may provide great information; but most people would probably not call him eloquent. In this case, the audience understands what is being said but they are not moved by how he says it. Reciprocally, a TED talk speaker may speak charismatically but not say anything particularly valuable. Again, he may not be considered eloquent because his content fails to live up to his style. Unlike these two examples, we want to strive for compelling substance *and* a riveting style. We should aim to engage audiences' heads and hearts simultaneously.

In the Middle Ages, philosopher Thomas Aquinas explained a similar relationship between the "intellect" and the "will." He suggests that the intellect fuels understanding while the will fuels desire. The intellect concerns knowledge, such as seeking what is good and true. Meanwhile, Aquinas determined that the will acts as "rational appetite" which carries out goodness and truth in respect to the desires (II-I.8.1). After all, desire motivates us to act. Since we cannot desire what we cannot understand, we must understand what we desire so that we can pursue our desire.

At a fundamental level, Aquinas defines healthy willful action as love. In his *Summa Theologica*, he defines love as charity (II-II.27.1), which is willing the good of other people for their own sake. Since time and attention are precious resources of our audiences, we are charitable when we respect our audience's time and attention. In short, if we use the time and attention of our audiences, it better be for charitable reasons. And at the very least, we can charitably give them an eloquent experience.

We know our own limitations because we live them out as individuals. Consequently, self-love or willing the good of *ourselves* can serve as a directional starting point toward how we "will the good of other people." Now, if a communicator wills the good of others to serve themselves, this is not "love" in the Thomist sense. However, self-love can still be useful. We do not understand others in a vacuum. Rather, we understand our audience's humanity because we understand our *own* humanity. We extend our self-knowledge toward others to better understand them. Therefore, love of other people is partially informed by our own self-love. Although this self-love position has received some criticism, Aquinas hints at this self-love. Therefore, the better that we know and love ourselves in a healthy and humble way, the better we can know and love our audiences. This can lead to ethical and eloquent communication. Basically, as we compose a presentation, we can think, "If I was in the audience, would I want to sit through this presentation?" Or as we compose an e-mail, we can think, "Would I want to read a three-paragraph e-mail, when a one-paragraph e-mail would do?" While our readers and listeners are different people than us, it can often guide our rhetorical decision making in a caring way.

These attitudes of love, hospitality, and charity inform classical and medieval attitudes. They can help insulate us from an overinflated ego. They sober us up from distorted visions of reality. These attitudes can help us ground our tactics as we move into the more practical chapters—beginning with Chapter 2.

Keys to Practical Eloquence

The rhetorical mindset is essential to being eloquent. Being ethically strategic with our communication feeds the rhetorical mindset.

In being strategic with our communication, seek to forecast futures by considering options and possible outcomes. By considering these options and outcomes, we weigh how different audiences react to our speaking or writing. We also trace how the circumstances may play a role in our rhetorical speech or writing.

The eloquent communicator adopts a charitable attitude. Accordingly, look to care for our listeners or readers. In doing so, we can consider we would appreciate if we were in their position. Beginning with a humble type of self-love can inform persuasive outward-facing communication.

CHAPTER 2

Trust the Trivium

When we sit down to write an e-mail, what are the first things we think about? What's our process? First, we probably consider which ideas we want to communicate. After that, we probably grab our laptop and begin typing. Words fly upon the screen as sentence units. These sentence units make up short paragraphs. Within these short paragraphs, we connect sub-ideas to main ideas to clarify our units of thought and why they make sense. At some point in the writing process—maybe toward the end—we may sit back and more specifically think about our reader. Will he or she understand what we are writing? Our words and ideas? Will they like our ideas? Will they like the way we wrote it? Will they be annoyed by anything? Considering these dimensions, we may return to the e-mail and change a word or two, or maybe add or delete an idea, until we finally click "send."

If we write in a similar process to this, we have consulted the classical trivium, the ancient (and medieval) foundation of the liberal arts. The trivium is composed of three intertwined dimensions of communication: grammar, logic, and rhetoric. Importantly, the dimensions are not mutually exclusive. Their overlap looks like this:

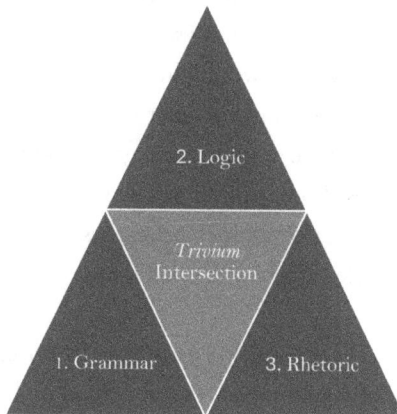

Figure 2.1 The trivium in the classical liberal arts tradition

The trivium composes a trifold interplay. The word trivium means the intersection of three roads. If we neglect even one of these dimensions, our communication fails. Therefore, effective communication, and *nimble* communication, in a very fundamental manner, considers all three. As we will discuss in this chapter, each pillar relies on the other pillars, but the first two (grammar and logic) are mastered by the third (rhetoric). Consequently, when a writer or speaker is good at an area of the trivium, it can "raise all ships." It elevates the effectiveness of the other two dimensions. And more negatively, when we fail at one, we "lower all ships." It negatively affects the other two.

So, what is the goal? We should be attentive to all of three. We should build habits that consider each of the three when we communicate to colleagues, clients, customers, and investors. After all, a solid foundation is crucial to the art of eloquence. The classical rhetoricians acknowledged these foundations as the bases of communication. If we celebrate and master the basics, then we build a solid construction.

By understanding each of these large levers in the communication machine, we can more fully wield its power and avoid pitfalls. So, let's consider each one in isolation before considering their interrelationships and how they benefit our business relationships.

Grammar: Commanding Our Symbols

First, let's think about grammar. But isn't a discussion of grammar far too basic? Especially when discussing professional communication? Didn't we learn grammar as a child in "grammar school"?

Grammar isn't as basic as we might think. By consulting the wisdom of older traditions, we can consider the wider and deeper dimensions of grammar. Classical understandings of grammar extend much deeper than mere rules about capitalization and punctuation. A classical consideration of grammar examines principles, not only rules. And if we ignore the principles of grammar, we ignore the cornerstone of the trivium.

So, what is classically understood grammar? In writing, it naturally involves mechanics like capitalization and punctuation, but it also involves appropriate parts of speech and language. When discussing thoughtful communication, Bonaventure, the classically informed Scholastic philosopher from the Middle Ages, explains that grammar allows audiences to apprehend an expressed message through its appropriateness or correctness. As such, rules of correctness help audiences apprehend the ideas expressed in the speaking or writing.

Considering modern business, we want our messages to be apprehended quickly. Therefore, our grammar should be crystal clear. That said, it would be babyish to review grammatical rules like the parts of speech and punctuation. Naturally, we should strive to write and speak grammatically correct to demonstrate an appreciation of order and radiate a professional ethos, which are both dimensions of persuasion. After all, do we trust someone with sloppy or negligent grammar? Probably not.

Moreover, the correctness of grammar helps quicken the reading or listening experience. That is, correct grammar helps readers or listeners not labor over our messages. As Edward Stull mentions in his book *UX Fundamentals for Non-UX Professionals*, modern audiences seek the least amount of work. They are conservative by nature. Because our audiences have presumably attended grade school and seen the patterns of (generally effective) grammar in the world, they will expect correct grammar from us. These are the expectations we are working with. Audiences will read or listen to our message more quickly if we satisfy their grammatical expectations. It is that simple. If we break those expectations, then our audience will work harder to reconfigure the patterns to apprehend the message. As Steven Krug discusses throughout his UX book, *Don't Make Me Think!*, users (or audiences in general) want to easily receive their experiences, *not accommodate* experiences. After all, accommodation takes work, energy, and time. And audiences find it annoying to spend extra energy and time, especially when they do not expect to.

The twentieth-century classical liberal arts scholar and teacher of trivium-based education Miriam Joseph defines grammar as "correctness" but also as "thing-as-it-is-symbolized." Centuries earlier, Augustine explained grammar as two types of "signs": (1) "given signs" and (2) "natural signs." "Given signs" are "those which living things give to each other, in order to show, to the best of their ability, the emotions of their minds, or anything they have felt or learnt" (2.3). These signs transport what is in one mind and deliver to another person's mind through the use of symbols (2.3). These "given signs" differ from the "natural signs." "Natural signs" organically unfold in nature, like footprints in sand that signify someone has walked by or smoke signifying fire. "Given signs" differ because they are deliberate *and* human. These two types of signs intersect because our given signs should correspond to the natural reality that surrounds us. To communicate well, we seek to place what is in our mind into the audience's mind. But importantly, the reality outside of us should initially inform what is in our mind—or else we will communicate fantastic fabrications or outright lies.

Therefore, the words we choose matter. Before we speak or write, we can consider the questions: What words should we select in our speaking or writing? Do they accurately portray the reality? Where do we place words in sentences so that the word order communicates something understandable?

So, on a basic level, do we call our customers "guests" or "giraffes"? Do our words, as symbols of things in reality, correctly depict the communicated reality? Do our words match our context? If we choose the word "guest" to describe our customers, does the implied connotation, such as hospitality, cooperate with our business? Or are we rhetorically stretching the grammar of customer as "guest" too much? Does "customer" as "guest" match the reality, say, in a retail store? Furthermore, will stretching the grammar confuse our customers? Will customers think: "Why am I being called a 'guest' in a store where I am buying a bed? This isn't Bed & Breakfast." Or will customers sense desperation? Will they think, "Man, they are so eager to appeal to me by using the word 'guest.' Are they struggling for business or something?" Or will customers see through the tactic and sense they are being manipulated by the grammar? Will they think: "I see what they are doing with the word 'guest.' They think they can confuse me into shopping here." In short, we must be careful when changing our language. Our audiences may pick up more than they let on.

Like many other retail outfits, the retail chain Target calls their customers "guests." In fact, employees ("Team Members") are required to refer to customers as "guests." Even if employees forget the language behind closed doors, managers ("Team Leads") will likely correct them. Team Leads must reorient the grammar of their fellow Team Members to craft a company narrative, and, ultimately, nourish the company culture. But at the root of this culture is specific Target language. For example, titles like Guest, Team Member, Team Lead, and ETL (Executive Team Lead) offer the grammar of Target. The grammar certainly offers rhetorical components, which will be discussed later; however, the roles enacted by customers and employees are labeled, and consequently influenced, by words. Employees may act more like a part of a team if they refer to themselves as "team members." "Guests" may feel like guests if employees refer to them as guests.

Now, words may be stretched but not neglected completely. If we neglect what words mean, we disconnect our language from reality. For instance, if Target required employees to refer to customers as "friends," it would probably be weird. For example, if employees greeted customers with, "How may I help you, friend?" or if "Guest Services" (which elsewhere is called "customer services") is retitled "Friend Services," the grammar would miss the mark. The effect: The language sounds too contrived and creepy. To call a customer, who is a stranger, a "friend" compromises the grammar and distorts reality.

It may seem basic, but it is important to know what words mean. As a human construction, language is never fully fixed as ancient Roman poet Horace observes in his *Ars Poetica*: "Many a word long dead will be born again, and others / which now enjoy prestige will fade, if Usage requires it" (lines 70–71). However, communication requires a stable language. Due to more relativistic attitudes toward language, language is more outwardly fluid than ever before in today's contemporary world. It doesn't help that the Internet disseminates ever-changing language trends. Now when language softens and shifts so often, it gives chances for people to confuse, mislead, or even manipulate others with language. So, we have to be careful. Presumably, we want our business to be sustainable (i.e., ethical), and we want to be seen as orderly and stable. We don't want to unintentionally mislead our colleagues, supervisors, or customers. Therefore, language should closely cooperate with understood meanings in respect to the reality outside of us.

Certainly, words never can fully capture reality because they are symbols. Consequently, it is important to know what we refer to, and that our references align with what audiences understand. After all, a single misstep in the correctness of a word can alter the meaning. A single misstep can undercut the confidence that listeners or readers have for us. For example, the word "invaluable" means indispensable. However, sometimes the word is used incorrectly assuming that, because of the prefix "in-," the word means "*not* valuable." This misstep can confuse readers of listeners because of the conflicting meanings. For instance, the sentence, "The product is not worth our time because it is invaluable" can leave a reader scratching their head. It contradicts itself. Ultimately, although words can change nuanced meaning over time, they still maintain stable meanings within moments of communication. Audiences appreciate the stability of language because it assists quick, clear communication.

To guide these decisions about grammar (i.e., the nature of specific things in respect to words), we can consult Aristotle's *Categories*. In this work, he provides a list of ten characteristics or "categories" to help us better understand "how particulars exist." Below is a chart of these natural traits of things:

CATEGORY	Description	Example #1	Examples #2
Substance	That which exists in itself	A person	Chair
Quantity	Giving it parts as distinct from its parts—a measurement	Tall	Four legs
Quality	Nature or form of substance	Handsome, intelligent, athletic	Brown
Relation	Reference bearing to another	Friend, near	Lower than the table
Action	Active power to produce effect in something else	Standing up, smiling	Carries heavy weight
Passion	Passive reception from another agent	Being invited to return, being drafted	Collapses under heavy weight
When (time)	Measure of duration of the substance	Sunday afternoon	The chair was built two days ago
Where (place)	Position in relation to things that surround the substance/ determine its place	On a bench, beside a lake	In the dining room
Posture	The parts of a substance have on each other	Sitting, leaning forward	Right-side up
Having	Clothing or ornaments that conserve the being or conserve the community that it is a part	In a grey suit	Covered in dust

Figure 2.2 Aristotle's "Ten Categories of Being"

While this chart may seem sophisticated, it is quite basic. It is sophisticated and basic. And it can give us a useful tool. If we are looking for the appropriate word to use, or a creative way to use words, we can look to these categories. It gives us a 360° understanding of the grammar in action much more than spinning our wheels with online dictionaries, thesauruses, or generative AI. So, if we are thinking about specific words in a marketing campaign, taglines, SEO terms, or even our own personal branding, Aristotle's categories may provide insights into how words are interpreted by our audiences.

After all, online dictionaries, online thesauruses, and generative AI bots do not actively live in the world. Therefore, these resources do not understand the living usage of words, specifically how living uses of words contrast and overlap poetical uses of words. In his work *Against Professors*, ancient Roman thinker Sextus Empiricus provides a popular definition of grammar as "knowledge of the forms of speech in the poets and also those in common usage" (Sect. 84). Sextus did not agree with this definition, but it works well for us. While various business writing textbooks and professional speaking handbooks discourage poetic communication tactics (which, consequently, limits communicators' rhetorical optionality), the rhetorically mindful classical tradition embraces optionality. It appreciates both literal and figurative uses of language. It appreciates common uses and poetical uses of language. And we can, too.

While literal and figurative uses of language will be fully taken up in the other sections of this book, it is worth pointing out that not all grammar operates the same way. Literal language directly represents things in the world, while figurative language provides a figure (such as a metaphor) that more obscurely represents things in the world in terms of other things. But it is crucial that our audiences understand the referents (things in the world) through our references (symbols used). To streamline this understanding, grammatical rules exist outside of the language itself but guide the use of words. These rules are important. The placement of words is important not just for emphasis (see "Style: Plain, Forceful, Middle, and Grand" section of Chapter 4) but also for clarity.

For example, a hotel manager seeks to place a sign in her hotel lobby about complementary coffee. Which one offers the clearest grammar?

Sentence #1: "Guests are welcome to free complimentary coffee."
Sentence #2: "Free complimentary coffee is welcome to guests."
Sentence #3: "Welcome, guest are, a complimentary: coffee to."

Of the two grammatically correct sentences (#1 and #2), the subject-to-object version ("Guests are welcome to free complimentary coffee") is the most direct sentence arrangement in English. It offers the most simple and direct grammar. It offers the quickest read. Clearly, the third option is the most difficult to read because it is grammatically incorrect. Therefore, the third sentence is the worst option. In fact, the manager may be better off not displaying a sign at all than displaying the third option.

In writing, punctuation rules seldom shift, especially in professional writing, because breaking the rules can obscure the meaning or slow down the uptake of the communication. Since speed is crucial to business communication, every second we lose on obscure sentence construction can damage relationships with readers. Therefore, although the 2020s have seen more frequent uses of comma splices, they (and other run-on sentences) should be avoided. That said, rules can be broken if the genre and the rhetorical situation allow for it. For example, we may be able to insert a sentence fragment into a document for emphasis. But it needs to work rhetorically. If our audience does not understand the sentence fragment, or they stumble over it and reread it, then it doesn't rhetorically work. In other words, if broken rules slow down our audiences in ways that frustrate them, then the broken rules do not work rhetorically.

Overall, for our purposes, grammar involves two dimensions: (1) choice of words in concordance with reality, and (2) rules that organize a quick and clear read or listen. Although we tend to love unabashed freedom in the 2020s, orderly rules do not inhibit freedom in the classical tradition. In fact, rules can allow us to be freer. In his 1908 book *Orthodoxy*, champion of classical education G. K. Chesterton shares an apt metaphor of children playing ball on an island of cliffs. If there are no walls on the edge of the island, the children cannot play ball as freely. With walls, however, the children can play ball much more freely. In this metaphor, he illustrates how too much freedom can restrict decision making and action. The rules of grammar act like island walls that allow us to "play ball" more robustly and freely. This celebration of constraints is endorsed in the modern era, as well. For example, in his 2013 book *The Laws of Subtraction*, professional creativity coach Matthew E. May admits and outlines how "creativity thrives under intelligent constraints." Grammar acts as such a constraining force to nourish creativity. After all, some of the most creative poetical minds, like Virgil, Dante, Shakespeare, John Milton, Emily Dickinson, T. S. Eliot, and others, did not throw out all of the rules and write poetry. As classically educated artists, they worked within the grammatical boundaries. While they broke some of the rules, they broke them with reality in mind, within moderation, and for audience-minded effect.

In short, we can become more eloquent in the workplace when we embrace classical grammar: figurative and literal uses of words, and the rules that guide the mechanics. Although rhetorical principles should fuel professional communication and playful uses of grammar, grammatical rules provide the stable guardrails that drive eloquent communication forward.

Logic: Uniting Our Ideas

Over 10 years ago, soon after graduate school, I interviewed for a full-time writing professor job in upstate New York. Since it was an on-campus interview, the chairman of the hiring committee, and veteran professor of writing, kindly took me out to lunch in between the day's events. He confessed that he was fascinated that I teach logic in my college writing classroom. He was curious, and a bit confused, about why I introduce logic into writing classes. I tried my best to mask my own confusion. I gently reminded him that the communication of ideas requires logic to work, and ancient thinkers recognized this thousands of years ago. But he still seemed to think that logic was exotic to writing. To this day, I'm still mystified by his reaction.

Unfortunately, logic is still neglected throughout American universities and professional communication training. Sure, logic can be difficult to learn, but it is essential to not only for some communication but *all* communication. As the ancient and medieval thinkers recognized, logic is a cornerstone of persuasion. In fact, Aristotle saw it as the "counterpart" of rhetoric. And logic does not only help us produce texts; it also helps how we receive other people's texts. After all, logical aptitude strengthens reading and listening skills, as well. Therefore, when we strengthen our habits of logic thinking, we become better writers/speakers and readers/listeners.

So, what is a basic definition of logic? How does it operate in communication? Miriam Joseph defines logic within the trivium as "thing-as-it-is-known" or thought about. This perspective differs from grammar ("thing-as-symbolized") because logic involves the process of thinking about ideas in relation to one another. While our ideas are expressed through language, logic concerns our ideas themselves.

And Joseph's perspective is not new. The classically influenced thinkers in the Middle Ages were fascinated by logic. They recognized that logic fuels our understanding of the world: both the physical sciences and the philosophical sciences. Many of these thinkers devoted time and effort into examining logic. Accordingly, some of these important figures share insightful definitions of logic. For example, John of Salisbury (riffing off of late antiquity thinker Boethius) defines logic as the "science of ... argumentative reasoning" in respect to verbal expression. Hugh of St. Victor further clarifies it as "clear-sighted argument that separates the true from the false." Bonaventure defines logic as the "principles of understanding" in relation to "judging" via "*true* speech." All three thinkers wrote extensively on logic—and how it informs communication and rhetoric.

Later, we will discuss the everyday facets of logic later as they directly connect to the persuasive power of dialectics, appeals to logos, and the invention process. But to understand how the logical machine operates and its importance to professional eloquence, let's examine a marketing example from history.

In the late 1800s, Ivory Soap ran a significant ad campaign. The campaign highlighted the soap's ability to float in water. And they promoted the buoyancy as a primary reason that customers should purchase it. After all, if a customer dropped the soap in the tub, they would not have to search underwater for the soap. Ultimately, the logic fueling of their advertisements was:

(Premise #1) If a soap floats, then it is a great soap.
(Premise #2) Ivory Soap floats.
(Conclusion) Therefore, Ivory Soap is a great soap.

By analyzing the logic alongside the grammar of these claims, we can recognize how this argument may not be as powerful as it may initially appear. The company portrayed an argument as sound when, in fact, the argument is only valid and not sound.

Now what are the differences between "valid" and "sound"? A valid argument proceeds in logical order. The Ivory Soap ad offers a particular logical organization known as *modus ponens*—one of the simplest structures, but still very useful. In it, Premise #1 plus Premise #2 equals a third term, a conclusion: (Premise #1).

The structure unfolds as follows:

(Premise #1) If A then B.
(Premise #2) A.
(Conclusion) Therefore, B.

It makes sense because the operations are valid: B necessarily follows from A; therefore, when A is supplied, B must be concluded.

While a valid argument offers logical operations, a *sound* argument offers a valid structure *in addition to* true information in the premises. When true premises are placed in a valid logical structure, the conclusion must be true.

A sound *modus ponens* argument may read as such:

(Premise #1) If Socrates is human then he is mortal.
(Premise #2) Socrates is human.
(Conclusion) Therefore, Socrates is mortal.

The structure is logically valid. And because the premises are true, the argument is also sound.

The Ivory Soap advertisement offers an interesting case because it uses the valid structure called *modus ponens*, but it does not communicate a particularly sound argument. To better understand its deficiency, classical grammar can be first analyzed. That is, we can analyze how the "things are symbolized" with words. We can analyze how grammar and logic must cooperate, or not cooperate, and evaluate the means of persuasion.

Clearly, premise #2 ("Ivory Soap floats") is accurate. After all, data/evidence supports that Ivory Soap floats in water. However, premise #1 ("If a soap floats, then it is a great soap"), the major premise, is trickier. The claim may be quickly assumed, but is it accurate? Let's first consider "soap" through Aristotle's previously mentioned ten categories. In the category of "action," soap cleans a person's body. We can reasonably assume that the cleaning power of soap is the primary reason why people purchase soap. Yet, in the Ivory advertisement, a category of "action," specifically that soap cleans, is being overlooked in favor of the "relative position" category, that the soap floats in water. The "relative position" category of floating is held as the most important criterion when assessing the soap. This raises some red flags. After all, shouldn't the "action" category should be used as the most important criteria? That is, should the soap be primarily assessed by how it cleans, *not* if it floats?

Let's continue the grammatical analysis. What about the word "great"? In respect to a commercial product, "great" often means that an object excellently performs its primary function. The word "great" grammatically differs from the word "unique." Ivory Soap's buoyancy makes it unique, but not necessarily "great." It is reasonable to assume that most people would think that "great" concerns the primary function of soap: to clean the human body. By understanding the categories of the nature of the soap, and how they are symbolized correctly (or incorrectly) through diction, the logic of this advertisement can be better understood. And we can better understand the deliberate misdirection in the marketing. After all, as Robert McPhee and Thomas Gerace point out in their book *Storynomics*, Ivory Soap knew that the product was not very good at cleaning the body. Therefore, Ivory focused on its relative position to water (floating) to misdirect and dazzle the public with a unique spectacle involving the soap. In a way, they muddled the word "great" with the word "unique" within their evaluative argument to misdirect customers away from Ivory Soap's weaker cleaning power.

Ultimately, logical instruction helps us think more clearly to communicate complex ideas to someone else. Along with grammar, it is the bedrock of communication; as such, logic is pivotal to eloquent communication.

Rhetoric: Persuading Our Public

At the age of 37, I arrived to teach at University of Providence in Great Falls, Montana. A few weeks in, I was speaking to a colleague about the central-north region of the state, where Great Falls was located. Soon, he became quite comfortable in our conversation. He shared that last year in his garage, "he dressed a six-point that he bagged before a chinook." I smiled and nodded. But I had no idea what he was talking about. Was he speaking another language?

Over the weeks, I picked up the context. I gathered the specifics through context clues about the words over time. After all, I vaguely knew about hunting culture. And Montana is *the* American state for hunting. Some of us who may hunt may know the terms. But for those of us who may not be familiar:

"Dressed" = Prepared the meat for storage

"Six-point" = Six pointed horns on a deer. Six-points signify that it is a large deer

"Bagged" = Killed and transported home

"Chinook" = Chinook winds, which are dry winds that blow down mountain ranges.

My colleague was being rhetorical for a Montanan speaking to another Montanan; however, I wasn't yet a Montanan. So, the rhetoric didn't work. I didn't understand the rhetorical grammar of the utterances. I also didn't the rhetorical logic of his assessment (why was bagging of the six-point a good thing?). I don't fault the man for speaking to me like a local Montanan. I took it as a compliment. After all, he spoke to me as if I had been accepted into Montanan culture. That said, if he was more audience-minded, he would have pivoted his grammar and logic toward my lack of Montana knowledge. And in doing so, he would be much more rhetorically effective.

Mindfulness toward audience is rhetorical mindedness. It emphasizes effective communication directed toward the public. Miriam Joseph aptly defines rhetoric as "thing-as-it-is-communicated" or outward-facing publicness. If our words and ideas effectively connect to our listeners or readers, then we are being rhetorically effective. And, of course, there are varying levels and dimensions of that connectivity to consider. We will consider them in forthcoming chapters.

Rhetoric fuels all effective communication. Yet, unfortunately, rhetoric is seldom discussed as rhetoric in the professional world. For example, In Daniel Pink's marketing book *To Sell Is Human*, Pink discusses "attunement." He defines attunement as "perspective-taking" which forms the "heart" of moving other people: "the ability to bring one's actions and outlook into harmony with other people and with the context you're in." Basically, he refers to thinking, acting, and communicating rhetorically. Ultimately, Pink's entire book is about rhetoric. So are many other important books on sales and persuasive communication.

When understanding effective professional communication as rhetorical communication, we should be careful not to make the common modern mistake of overspecializing or breaking things up without acknowledging the cooperative elements of the trivium. Modern thinkers often dissect things into parts but then leave the parts on the laboratory table. They tend to cut things into smaller and smaller pieces. For instance, while *Storynomics* is a great book, McKee and Gerace make this common modern mistake. They separate rhetoric from logic when they describe advertisements as being *either* rhetorical *or* logical. This binary separation is anathema to a classically minded thinker, and not very productive. The classical tradition, on the other hand, is much more synthetic and constructive. It considers *both/and* relationships, rather than *either/or* relationships. It considers how everything works together, including rhetoric, logic, and grammar. To its advantage, it works more holistically. After all, while a text may emphasize rhetoric or logic more than another text, as the trivium suggests, rhetoric is essentially tethered to logic whenever logic is communicated.

Yet the rhetorical communicator does not only know when to communicate the logic but also when *not* to communicate the logic. For example, imagine that we are pitching a new business to investors. As part of our pitch, do we need to persuade them about the value of money? Do we need to justify why profits are good? Generally, no. But both points are crucial parts of the pitch. However, we can assume that the investors understand these basic points and leave them out. Therefore, we decide not to communicate part of the logic without betraying the logic itself.

This removal is a rhetorical maneuver. It considers the audience, while at the same time, it stays true to the logic itself.

Overall, rhetoric savors optionality. Rhetoric seeks the best possible purpose-driven option for the audience and the circumstance. Aristotle's definition "the faculty of observing in any given case the available means of persuasion" unites grammar with logic and directs it toward a public in a mission-driven manner. As such, Miriam Joseph qualifies rhetoric as the "master art of the trivium," since it "presupposes and makes use of grammar and logic." Rhetoric is a unifier. It unifies the message. It unifies the speaker to the listeners. It unifies the writer to the reader. And to do this with artistry and mastery, we become eloquent.

Keys to Practical Eloquence

Grammatically incorrect sentences, which are mismarked or misarranged in writing or in speech, require higher cognitive loads from audiences. They require effort and waste time which can be frustrating. Therefore, try to avoid these missteps.

Grammatical order is appreciated (but likely not explicitly celebrated) by readers and listeners. Remember, people remember mistakes more than correctness. Let's make sure that our writing and speaking are grammatically correct so that people do not remember us by our mistakes.

The symbols should match the shared reality between communicator and audience. The better we know the world around us and respective linguistic options, the better we can symbolize the world around us.

Consider the logic of the communicated ideas. How to the ideas relate to one another? Will audiences understand these relationships? Which parts of the logic can be left out to be more efficient?

Recognize that language, logic, and audience awareness all cooperate. To be eloquent, seek to harmonize all three dimensions.

CHAPTER 3

Aims of Eloquence

When we strategize, our goals keep us on task. Like any journey toward a destination, our endpoint steers us in the right direction. Its orients our activity. The same applies to eloquent communication. Before we speak or write, we should consider our desired endpoints: What do we want our audience to leave our interaction with? How do we want them to feel? Empowered? Encouraged? Thoughtful? What common experience do we want craft and share?

We can influence others in a variety of ways. We can teach or coach them. We can move or motivate them. We can delight or entertain them. But what if I said that we don't have to pick one? What if we can do all three? This catch-all approach is what classical rhetoricians Cicero, Augustine, and Quintilian call for: The eloquent speaker or writer intersects all three aims. The eloquent communicator teaches, moves, and delights. Of course, one of these aims likely focuses on the communication. But the other two aims don't necessarily dissolve completely away. Each of the three overlaps and cooperates. As such, they engage our audience holistically. They engage the head, heart, and senses.

Before considering this cooperation, let's look at how each aim operates and consider some specific tactics.

Instruct the Intellect

Teaching well is not reserved only for professional teachers or trainers. It is a skill essential to all effective communication. Ultimately, all communication conveys information and seeks that audiences understand thought; therefore, all communication teaches in some manner. When we tell our husband or wife about our day at work, we convey information. Even when placing our order at Burger King or Taco Bell, we instruct the drive-thru employee about specific order preference.

However, teaching does more than merely share information. When we share information, we focus on "what-content," which is fairly basic. Teaching a craft or skill is more advanced. I think we can agree that teaching a child how to ride a bike is more complex communication than placing an order at Burger King. While teaching an ability may refer to "what-content," it primarily focuses on how to do something or "how-content." Finally, when we teach knowledge or wisdom, we focus on deeper philosophies or "why-content." Ultimately, effective teachers recognize and toggle the interplay of these three levels: the what, how, and why. And as eloquent communicators, we should too.

The "what," "why," and "how" fuel good teaching. And we can share each of these in any order. After all, the order depends on our specific audiences and circumstances. For example, if our audience doesn't know foundational contexts, terms, or ideas, we should probably teach the "what" before getting into the "how" and "why." While this sounds basic, it requires judgment and vigilance. Therefore, the eloquent communicator accurately *reads* the audience's proficiency level. Or if they are familiar with the audience, they *remember* what the audience may or may not know. Then, accordingly, they use what the audience *does know* to guide them toward what they *don't know*.

For example, our workplace team may know the company's projection numbers from previous year, but they don't know the projection numbers just released for this upcoming year. Before we share the new data, we may decide to remind the team about last year's data. While the team is familiar with old information, the reminder is appreciated. When we present the new information, they compare the new numbers with the old numbers to contextualize what the new information means. Ultimately, we bridge from what they *do* know to what they *don't* know. The move is simple, comfortable, and accordingly effective.

Then, we may explain "why" the "what" matters. Why does the newly shared information make things easier or more effective for our audience? Why does it make the business stronger as a whole? For example: we may want to explain *why* this year's projection numbers are important. And stepping back even further, we can further explain why projection numbers are important in general. By emphasizing the significance of the "what," our audience becomes more invested in what is being taught.

Finally, we may want to explain "how" the new knowledge or skills can be implemented in the workplace: the practical tactics, moments, and places. If we have the time and resources, we may even have our audience test out the "how" in a low-stakes manner before they use them in the world. Perhaps we can talk though case studies or perhaps facilitate hands-on training activities. This way, our audience can feel more confident and comfortable in applying the "how" in the world. In respect to the projection numbers example, we can explore how the team can boost the low projection numbers. How can the organization be more assertive? How can individual contributions make the company more assertive in the marketplace? And, if the projection numbers are high, how can the organization sustain such growth?

While the projection number example moved from "what" to "why" to "how," these three ingredients can be arranged differently. For example, Steve Jobs' keynote presentations were often arranged as "why," "what," and then "how." When introducing the iPod in 2007, he first why Apple's innovations are important, then he introduced what the iPod is, and finally he discussed how it worked. In short, there is no formula to follow because it depends on our message, audience, and occasion, but the three categories can usefully structure how we teach others.

Overall, an informed teacher instructs concepts and information, the reasoning behind concepts and information, *and* ways to act upon them in the world. By reinforcing the practical tactics, our "students" build actionable habits. Therefore, passive memorization alone is generally insufficient. Instead, we should strive to get our audiences to actively apply particular knowledge or recognize its practical utility. In short, emphasizing both the "why" and the "how" allows teachers to optimize learning. As virtually all business communication experts advise, we should help our audiences understand "What's in it for me": useful applicable knowledge.

Communicating our ideas as painkillers helps emphasize the urgency of the "what's in it for me." Charisma coach Vanessa Van Edwards explains that "painkiller" ideas immediately relieve problems. They provide practical solves. "Painkillers" differ from "vitamins." Like actual vitamins, vitamin ideas can be good to our audience's "health." While vitamin ideas can be great, they take time to heal things. Vitamin ideas do not immediately solve pressing issues. While both types of ideas contribute to the persuasive utility of the "what's in it for me," painkiller ideas are often more appreciated by audiences because they supply relief. Consequently, they are more persuasive than vitamin ideas.

Teaching the "how" (i.e., hands-on practice, skill, or habit) centers on *praxis*. *Praxis* is the ancient Greek concept of thoughtful or theory informed practical action. Centering on "doing," *praxis* is often viewed as the counterpart to *phronesis*, or practical wisdom. While *praxis* teaches the "how," *phronesis* teaches the principles or the "why" behind the practical decisions. So *phronesis* unfolds throughout liberal arts classrooms and philosophical discussions. But *phronesis* also unfolds out in the professional world. After all, principled "whys" deeply inform all types of actions. When we stay at work past 5 p.m. on a Friday, we do so for a reason. When we help a friend move into their new apartment, we do so for a reason. When we stick to our convictions during a negotiation, we do so for a reason.

As an instructional piece of communication, this very book *Influence with Eloquence* operates within these two distinctions of *phronesis* and *praxis*. The Introduction chapter and Chapter 1 focused more on *phronesis*, while Chapter 2, this chapter, and subsequent chapters explore *praxis*. That said, this split is not exclusive. Like the ancient rhetorical handbooks of Aristotle, Cicero, and Quintilian, *praxis* and *phronesis* work together throughout the chapters of this book: since well-rounded eloquent communication depends on both. Both theory and practice matter.

Unlike today's modern attitudes, ancient tradition is not strictly driven by utility. This pill may be difficult to swallow in the modern result-oriented marketplace. This modern orientation may see experience as the coin of the realm. When communicating instructively, we must be careful not to fall into that trap. We can emphasize personal experience too much. It can lead us astray. Contemporary philosopher Nassim Taleb points this out throughout much of his literature. He emphasizes the seemingly basic (but often forgotten) point that if an individual sees a particular pattern, it does not necessarily make it universally true. If someone only sees white swans, it does not mean that black swans do not exist. Our senses can deceive us about the truth. After all, black swans *do* exist. If half of a stick is submerged in water, the stick may seem bent, but it is not. What we see through the water's distortion is not the reality of the stick. Along those lines, personal experience does not automatically lead to wisdom.

Ultimately, while hands-on practice is important, the classical tradition demands that *phronesis* should be consulted. This perspective appreciates truths that have been verified not just by us, but by other authorities over thousands of years. Some claims have been handed down to us. And these claims still ring true. The classical and medieval traditions both applaud how the inheritance of wisdom results in wise teaching. While the present and future matter, these traditions insist that the past matters too.

How do these insights about both *praxis* and *phronesis* help us teach eloquently as modern professionals? The Greek terms for the study of effective education is "pedagogy." In Greek, the term means "the leading of children." Clearly, as business professionals, we do not teach children. However, it can be advantageous to embrace this ancient meaning of the term. After all, when leading others to understanding, it can be useful to slow down our reasoning. Sometimes it is useful to consider our professional audiences as novices, much like children.

I know that it may seem like terrible advice to treat our colleagues and customers as "children." But hear me out. Let's look to the wisdom of Augustine of Hippo, specifically his book entitled *For Instructing the Uninstructed* from 406 CE. He provides tactics about how to instruct others who may not possess the expertise we do. His topic still resonates today. After all, professionally, we often instruct others who are not experts in our field, branch, or area of specialization. While it may seem that we slowly explain topics like we speak with children, we can embrace such basic instruction. We should continue to communicate slowly and carefully. Why? Because we care for our listeners or readers who are not experts. If we do it well, Augustine says, we become "united with them … in heart"; as such, the material will seem new and exciting to us because *we see it freshly through their eyes* (Sect. 17). Much like children light up because they are excited and filled with wonder by the world around them, we can tap into this excitement, and consequently, awaken this excitement in our audience. By exciting our audience, we contagiously feel the same excitement. According to Augustine, teaching in this manner is like walking through the streets of a familiar city. When we encounter someone who is distressed because they do know where to go, we cheerfully direct them in the right direction (Sect. 17). It is the same feeling. Have you ever been approached by a stranger in a familiar city who asked for a restaurant recommendation? And since you know the city, you are happy to recommend a restaurant with care, charity, and cheer? This same feeling is endorsed by Augustine. And it is a similar approach to leading a child in the right direction.

However, when conveying expert knowledge, we should be careful of perfectionism. Because we know a subject well, we may feel confident that we can deliver a pitch or write an e-mail in an eloquent, clearer, or moving manner. Yet we sometimes still fall short a little bit. We may not match our ideal. It can be frustrating. And Augustine recognizes this. It frustrates him too. He feels distraught when his tongue betrays his heart. He becomes frustrated when his expression fails to communicate what he actually thinks and feels (Sect. 3). Yet, to repeat, teaching is not about us; it is about caring for our audience. Augustine explains that when we see that our audience is even remotely interested in our speech or writing, we should recognize that our speech may not be as "frigid" as we originally thought (Sect. 4). Audiences can still find our speaking or writing eloquent because they have no idea how much more eloquent it could have been. So don't let it discourage us. Conversely, we can recognize the glass half-full. Others have found value in our instruction. Focus on the positivity. It can become our solace. Therefore, even if we miss a chance to incorporate that clever metaphor, polished phrasing, or compelling idea, our audience never has to know about our initial plan. Most likely, they'll still find our communication interesting without that clever metaphor, polished phrasing, or compelling idea. So, while we want to be *perfective* as eloquent communicators, we don't want *perfectionism* to damage our basic teaching.

Move the Will

To move or motivate our audience, we should consider the relationship between teaching and moving. In a 2001 interview, Jeff Bezos exclaimed that "teachers who are really really good" "recognize their students" and "they create an environment where you can be very satisfied by the process of learning that's going on"; he explains,

> the great teachers, somehow convey, in their attitude and in their words and their actions and everything they do that this is an important thing you're learning and by doing that, you end up wanting to do more of it and more of it and more of it. I think that is a real talent. ... to convey the importance and reflect it back to the students.

Ultimately, Bezos says that great teachers do more than convey content to students. They electrify students about the importance and value of content. And this electricity is a fundamentally human (not AI) and live (not online) experience. We, as teachers, need to feel this excitement to properly convey it. After all, if we don't feel excited about the content, how do we expect to make our audience excited about it? This clearly goes for speaking, but it can also be conveyed in writing. Our excitement and passion can shine through our writing, too. But again, we must be excited about the content in the first place. Overall, effective teaching requires moving the will; reciprocally, the moving of the will requires good teaching.

In addition to the contagious excitement about the material itself, how do we substantively inspire audience to want to listen to us? Business consultant Simon Sinek explains that conveying the "why" behind something inspires people. A communicator who moves others doesn't just state facts and outline how to do something. Even if they are excited about facts and procedures, such content will not have lasting power. In addition to the passion, they need to express why it matters if their listeners or readers are to believe in the underlying values.

To illustrate the point, Sinek uses an analogy of dating, specifically through a hypothetical scenario. In a failed first date, a man merely tells the woman what his job is and how he does it. We can contrast that to a successful date where a man discusses the values of his profession and why it matters to him personally. In the first case, he simply relays information to the woman. In the second date, he communicates personal motivations about his values—what can't merely Googled, what requires meaningful conversation. These revelations about his drives inspire because they connect more intimately to a real person who lives out those values in the world. As Sinek claims, understanding the "why" is what makes someone charismatic, interesting, and ultimately, motivates people to want to understand.

Sinek explains that moving the will does not only require charismatic energy (although charismatic energy helps), but it requires the "why" that justifies belief. The clarity of the belief and the "why" becomes crucial to moving an audience member's will. In other words, it is not enough for us to say that we participate in beach cleanups in Naples, Florida, every weekend; instead, the action needs to be connected to the logic. We need to explain the reasoning that supports our motives toward the action. We might want to share how beach cleanups connect us with nature, remind us of our childhood, or inspire optimism. After our partner understands the "why," they are then equipped to act on it themselves. Of course, as bonus, they will probably find us more interesting and worth conversing with. As such, the instructive purpose connects, and pivots toward, moving the will.

We should stoke the desire in our audiences if we want them to keep listening or reading. This can be tough because attention spans have shrunk so much in the last 50 years. Still, audience attention has always been an issue, even back in Augustine's time. Augustine explains,

> It is likewise a frequent occurrence that one who at first listened to us with all readiness, becomes exhausted either by the effort of hearing or by standing, and now no longer commends what is said, but gapes and yawns, and even unwillingly exhibits a disposition to depart. (Sect. 19)

To this, he tells us that it is our "duty to refresh his mind". We can share something unique, astonishing, or cheerful to win back their will (as long as it connects to the discussion, of course). While still being friendly, we can share something grim and painful as well, to awaken their attention, if, of course, it doesn't offend them (Sect. 19).

As Augustine suggests (and we have discussed earlier), we should be flexible. To move the will, we must recognize the present state of our audiences' will and move it from that state. Audiences may be in different states when we encounter them. They may be fatigued, agitated, energetic, or excited. Moreover, during our talk, or over the course of our writing, we may nudge them from their original positions. They may *become* fatigued, agitated, energized, or excited over the course of our communication. We may be able to predict these shifts, but other times we may not.

For example, during one recent semester, I spoke about the difficulties of the job market to sophomores and juniors at my university. They immediately became anxious and defensive. This reaction is understandable. It is an anxious topic. They folded their arms and shifted uncomfortably in their seats. When I noticed their reaction, I shifted my tone and delivery to become more lighthearted. This helped offset the gravity of the topic and balance the conversation. I had to click the rhetorical mindset into overdrive and trigger a real-time shift to balance and accommodate the students. It worked. The students became noticeably less closed off, and more receptive of the discussion. By working with audiences, rather than working against them, we can teach more effectively and move their will toward the subject matter so that they want to learn and put that learning into action.

Since we can only predict how an audience may react, we should be flexible to shift gracefully. We should probably have several options on hand. As stated previously, the rhetorical mindset, and, ultimately, eloquence, concerns optionality. We should prepare this optionality beforehand and overprepare an abundance of material. That way, if we need to pivot, we can. Moreover, we should become comfortable with letting parts of our talk go. If we don't get to them, it is fine. We can share that information next time, tell our team after the presentation, or mention it in a follow-up e-mail. In the realm of writing, we should likewise become comfortable with cutting parts of our writing. We can be flexible and discerning enough to recognize what flows naturally with the vibe of our readers and, contrarily, what can feel forced or redundant. This way, we do not seek to hammer a square peg into a round hole. This way, we work with our audience's energy, not against it.

To move others' wills, it takes strategic planning which involve potential contingency plans. For example, I teach 1-hour and 45-minute class sessions at Ave Maria University. I prepare about two and a half hours of material. About 95 percent of the time, I don't use this extra material. But, about 5 percent of the time, I am happy that I have extra material. It gives me the option to pivot if my students aren't connecting with something. In addition to teaching, I have also led professional training and coaching sessions. In 2020, I was hired to lead an online training session on persuasive reasoning for a government organization. The training had to be 4 hours. But I didn't prepare for a 4-hour session; instead, I prepared for a 5-hour session, which included an entire 20 slide deck that I never used. But since I didn't know what to expect, I prepared for the possibility of bad reception. As the old saying goes, I hoped for the best but prepared for the worst. If I read the online room and noticed people "gaping and yawning," I had backup material cued up to "refresh their minds" and reengage their interest. Luckily, I didn't have to use the extra slides. But I am happy that I had them.

If we are looking for some easy bonus material that can help move our audience, we should consider discussion questions. We can prepare discussion questions spark conversations with our audience. This way we can open up channels of discourse. Again, we may use discussion questions, or we may not. But they can be useful to have just in case. Again, if we need to pivot from our traditional presentation to an active discussion forum (or if our presentation is losing steam), we can pivot with confidence. While discussion forums may make us anxious because we place presentation in other people's hands, discussions inevitably interest audiences. An active discussion invites audiences into the conversation. Audiences are moved to learn because they become invested in the discourse. Audience members now have skin in the game. And, if we are nimble enough, we can still hit our talking points when leading a discussion forum. Asking questions to an audience is essentially a way to get feedback on ideas and learn about the audience. And, if things get too far off track, we can always corral their responses back to our original talking points. This overall feedback loop channels back into our rhetorical mindset. It helps us become more charitable and present *with* our audience, rather than *to* our audience.

Hands-on activities are a final way to engage the audience. This may seem like a grade school tactic. I get it. But bear with me. Again, we don't always need a hands-on activity. But it is a wonderful option if we have a sleepy or nonresponsive audience. It can be as simple as a "quick show of hands" poll to get the audience moving. Or it can consist of a more involved "talk to a neighbor for two minutes about the topic" or "a two-minute brainstorm jot on a piece of paper." The key is to get the audience apply content in a practical manner. People learn better and see the relevance of material when they do something with it. The relevance moves them to care about the material. But I must share a word of caution. I have worked with professionals in the field of education, and they tend to rely heavily on hands-on activities. Offering too many activities, especially in professional forums, become pedantic and feel like a waste of time. So, we should probably be sparing with these activities.

Does the classical tradition support such active learning? In *Nicomachean Ethics*, Aristotle explains that some faculties naturally occur, such as seeing and hearing. For other faculties, such as virtuous habits of mind and the arts, he offers a paradoxical relationship. He claims that we must learn some things before we do them well, but that, of course, requires that we learn by doing them (1103a33-34). He further specifies, "we become builders, for instance, by building, and we become harpists by playing the harp. Similarly, then, we become just by doing just actions. Temperate by doing temperate actions, brave by doing brave actions" (1103a35-1103b2). Therefore, the modern expression "Those that can't do, teach" is not classically minded. The expression can be revised in the classical tradition to say, "Those that *can't* do, teach *poorly*; those that *can* do, teach *well*." We can implement this type of active learning into our teaching. Once they understand, we can motivate our audience to act if we get them to practice the material and build habits of mind.

Delight the Senses

We live in an attention economy. Attention is a scarce resource in today's digitally saturated world, where we are bombarded with an overwhelming amount of information competing for our limited attention spans. And as contemporary rhetorician Richard Lanham tells us in his book *The Economics of Attention*, the ancients ultimately recognized rhetoric as the craft of getting and keeping people's attention. It was important in the ancient world—and it still is today. Because of such rampant stimuli, managing people's attention is even more important today than in the past. Grabbing our audience's attention through dazzle or delight, and maintaining that dazzle or delight throughout the composition or experience, acts to effectively corral their attention and direct it to the other two aims: to instruct and to move.

In his *Ars Poetica*, one of the first preserved guides that we have on poetry, ancient Roman poet Horace outlines the principles of effective poetry. In it he explains that poetry should be *utile et dulce*: both "useful" (*utile*) in teaching readers and "sweet" (*dulce*) in delighting readers. We can direct a similar attitude toward workplace writing and speaking. While we previously discussed the importance of teaching the intellect and moving the will, we should ensure that our writing or speaking is "sweet" as well as useful. In Book One of his *Satires*, Horace additionally explains that "what harm can there be in presenting truth with a laugh …?" (also translated: "What prevents us from *speaking truth with a smile?*"). Even teachers, he explains, give treats or cookies to their young students to help them learn the alphabet. The same principle applies to influential eloquence. We can give our audience positive gifts, something small like a joke, a smile, or even an optimistic perspective on an issue, or something more tangible like a useful handout or our deck of slides that we present on. Or maybe, as salespeople are urged to do, we distribute bottles of water to our audience. Or, as Horace suggests, literally give them cookies.

When we eliminate appearances of anxiety, we invite the possibility of more delightful communication experiences. This applies to speaking and writing. After all, audiences don't like encountering anxious people. Why? Because it makes them feel anxious, too. While it is common for speakers and writers feel some anxiety when communicating (because we want to do well), we should keep in mind that delightful experiences feel natural, not artificial. We want to cooperate with audiences, not steamroll over them. Overpreparing can help alleviate our anxiety because it provides some backup plans if things go belly-up.

As stated in previous chapters, Aristotle rightly claims that the art of rhetoric concerns optionality. The art of rhetoric helps us appropriately choosing from those options. Therefore, we want to have some options.

By thoroughly preparing our speech, meeting, or writing beforehand, we fully consider a range of relevant content and methods to communicate the content. In this way, we reduce the need to think on our feet. This preparation manifests itself as confidence, which is inherently persuasive and delightful. Because we control our anxiety, we can exude much more positivity and presence with our audience.

True presence involves being attuned to an audience, reading the room, and adapting our delivery as needed. This can be as simple as using audience members' names and acknowledging their specific situations, which makes them feel special and valued. As Robert Cialdini explains in his book *Influence: The Psychology of Persuasion*, making people feel good is paramount. Backed by studies, he simply observes that people prefer to say yes to people who they like. Being a positive presence helps in this regard, as people naturally gravitate toward those who make them feel good. Olivia Fox Cabane echoes this sentiment throughout *The Charisma Myth*, where she ultimately argues that we become charismatic when we feel good about ourselves because that internal positivity and confidence manifests outwardly to others. As such, we become attractive. This attractiveness is a beneficial by-product of the "self-love" that we discussed in Chapter 1. In short, the first step to get audiences to feel good about themselves is to model that positivity.

Confidence, therefore, radiates positivity. Just as optimism is contagious, so is confidence. When we project confidence, our audience is more likely to feel confident as well, especially if we are instructing or motivating them. Cabane emphasizes that confidence, optimism, and presence are the cornerstones of charisma. She notes that being present in a specific moment in time with another person makes us feel special and makes them feel special too. We bond and connect over the shared moment. As will be discussed in the section on delivery, it can be a reason why strangers connect so strongly and quickly in times of crisis. In short, overpreparing helps to build the confidence that makes our communication persuasive and delightful. By combining confidence with optimism and presence, we not only enhance our charisma but also make our audience feel good, which may not be the primary goal of the communication, but it can bridge toward our goals of instruction and persuasion.

In addition to optimism, confidence, and presence, we can delight and dazzle through our content. Specifically, we can delight through concrete examples, specifics, and particulars. These details are not only easier for audiences to understand, and audiences feel positively affirmed when they understand and follow them, but images and things are more connective and comfortable than abstract and vague concepts. We have different types of specifics to choose from as long as audiences can follow how the specifics connect to our logic. For example, stories are wonderful concrete ways to support our purpose or argument. After all, stories and anecdotes operate as examples that *show*, not merely *tell*. And the narratives engage the imagination. We will more deeply discuss the persuasive power of stories in Chapter 6 on storytelling.

In addition to stories, we can use metaphor. In *Poetics*, Aristotle proclaims that "the greatest thing by far is to have command of the metaphor" (1459a). He goes further to say that "it is a mark of genius" (1459a). In Book Three of *Rhetoric*, Aristotle celebrates metaphors because they hit all three rhetorical aims: they instruct, move, and delight. Moreover, metaphors communicate in fresh ways. For example, it is much more vivid to say: "Our HR director cared for us like a mother hen" than "Our HR director cared for us a lot." Due to its freshness, metaphor can grab the audience's attention. It also provides that delightful specificity by giving them images. Metaphors engage the imagination by painting a picture of something in their mind's eye.

Metaphors invite listeners or readers into the text as participants. And the more interesting and appropriate the metaphor, the more they delight audiences. Aristotle explains that metaphors allow listeners to be pleasantly surprised (1412a18-28). This happens because the audience realizes they have learned something differently—through a unique image and comparison—from what they initially thought, which leads to an internal reaction of, "That's so true! I never thought of it in that way!" Clever sayings are effective because the speaker uses figures, or figurative language to mean something different from the literal words used. Aristotle explains that figures behave like riddles in a way. Similarly, well-crafted riddles are enjoyable because understanding them involves a moment of insight. This enjoyment arises when the statement is unexpected and challenges the listener's preconceived notions. Like the joy found in solving riddles or puzzles, metaphors provide similar joy, albeit in a quicker way.

So, metaphors assist learning, but they also act as playful riddles to draw readers into texts. Metaphorical content teaches in memorable manners and the playful deceit delights readers. Lush metaphors also engage the imagination through mental "image making." As Longinus points out, the "imaginative pictures" helps "conceal the actual argument by its own brilliance." Arguments that "tell" rather than "show" can be too dry. Poetic use of metaphor within argument can be much more dazzling and delightful. It "shows" as a means to "tell."

Jeff Bezos loves to use metaphor. Bezos often emphasizes that Amazon should always operate with the enthusiasm and urgency of a startup, as if it were still "Day 1." This metaphor encourages employees to stay innovative and avoid complacency. In his 2016 shareholder letter, Bezos writes, "Day 2 is stasis, followed by irrelevance, followed by excruciating, painful decline, followed by death. And that is why it is always Day 1." Among his many other metaphors, he also uses the term "Two-Pizza Teams." This metaphor refers to Bezos's principle that workplace teams at Amazon should be small enough to be fed with two pizzas. This ensures that teams are agile, and communication is efficient. Bezos advocates for small, autonomous teams to foster innovation and speed. He explains, "No team should be so large that it cannot be fed with two pizzas."

Part of metaphor's effectiveness is that it works from the senses and guides audiences toward the abstract. Thomas Aquinas recognizes this when he discussed the senses in his *Summa Theologica*. Aquinas views sensory perception as a way to guide higher forms of intellectual understanding. Aquinas explains that the senses can help guide our intellect to know material objects, while our intellects alone understand the deeper nature of things (I.84.1-7). While sensory perception leads individuals to a preliminary understanding of the external world, we grasp deeper natures through intellectual reflection and reasoning.

Here, Aquinas borrows from the classical tradition, specifically Aristotle, with these insights. In *On the Soul*, Aristotle explains that senses work like a signet ring making an impression in wax: "just as the wax receives the impression of the signet-ring without the iron or the gold, and receives the impression of the gold or bronze, but not as gold or bronze" (424a).

Similarly, the senses give us an impression and allow us to grasp the external world, but it is ultimately the intellect that comprehends the deeper understanding of things.

Overall, the senses act as accessible entry points for audiences. This is why Steve Jobs relies so heavily on memorable images in his keynote presentations. This is why Jeff Bezos relies so heavily on stories and metaphors. This is why effective websites heavily rely on high-res photos. And this is also why our resumes should be cleanly designed. This is why we should dress well at job interviews. This is why we should carefully consider our backgrounds during video calls (and not blur them out). By engaging the senses, whether visually through images, metaphors, storytelling, or even through attire or environment, we create spaces that foster receptivity and enhance the message. When our audience is captivated and delighted, they are more likely to receive our message and *want* to receive our message. This leads to clearer judgment, open collaboration, and, ultimately, achieving goals in the workplace.

When we stimulate our audience' senses, we unlock a willingness to learn and be motivated. This openness is especially crucial today with so many distractions competing for people's attention. If we don't captivate and delight our audience through their senses at the beginning of an experience, it becomes more of a challenge to teach or influence them in broader ways. That said, it is also important to handle this delight carefully to ensure that it's not overdone. If we reveal our methods too soon, we become a magician revealing how their tricks work. The magic is lost. So, we should look to keep our audience consistently enchanted, creating a sequence of lasting impressions that will be fondly remembered. Much like Steve Jobs orchestrated in his Apple product release keynote presentations, if we sufficiently enchant our audiences, they will happily look forward to hearing us, speaking with us, and doing business with us again.

Bring It Together

In *De Optimo Genere Oratorum* (1.3-4), Cicero explains that the eloquent speaker in the Senate should teach, move, and delight in all of their speeches. Gesturing to Cicero, Augustine repeats this advice in Book Four of *De Doctrina Christiana*: the eloquent preacher should also teach, move, and delight. Business communication, while presumably distant from the statehouse or the pulpit, should heed this advice as well. Every effective piece of communication should fulfill these three purposes in some way. How well we do them may be a different story. Yet we can still seek to harness these purposes in every piece communication, whether selling a product, explaining an operation, or telling an anecdote to a client. Ultimately, to be influential, we should manage our audience's attention, mental understanding, and motivation toward action.

Teaching, moving, and delighting are part of a three-in-one or "tripartite" structure. Each can work within a text or speech to craft an effective piece of communication. Now, we can certainly emphasize or prioritize one of the three aims, but the other two aims should support that primary aim. For example, if we report on a new competitor in the marketplace, we will need to teach our team about the competitor. Then secondarily, we may move the team to see the company as a threat to our market share. The third priority, we can subtly weave delight into the report presentation experience via colorful document design and visuals, so our audience stays engaged and optimistic.

Let's think about a different example. At an after-work get-together, we tell a humorous story about tripping over a paint can in our garage. Our primary aim may be to entertain our coworkers and amuse them. Yet a by-product of the story may be that it teaches and inspires them to be aware of their surroundings. Moreover, the self-deprecating nature of the joke may also persuade them of our humility. That said, when we tell funny stories, we look to entertain our audience and make them laugh, not to present a lesson or persuade others. In fact, a lesson or moral may reduce a story's humorous effect. But, as always, it depends on the context, content, and audience. In sum, even if it seems like our story, presentation, or e-mail only has one purpose, other minor modes of persuasion still operate beneath the surface without us fully recognizing them. An eloquent communicator, however, recognizes these operations. They amplify or diminish the supplementary aims in accordance with his or her priorities.

When we harmonize all three aims, we engage the whole person. In his works like *Republic* and *Phaedrus*, Plato proposed that the soul consists of three parts: mind, spirit, and body. This trifold contrasts with the more modern (and arguably less complex) view of "I think, therefore I am" (*cogito ergo sum*) that has been handed down from Enlightenment philosopher René Descartes. Despite its name, "the Enlightenment" unfortunately led us toward a reductive understanding of the human person. Accordingly, it led to a reductive understanding of communication. "Cogito ergo sum" promotes the idea that humans are merely mind and body, akin to machines. In contrast, Plato, along with thinkers from the ancient world, Middle Ages, and Renaissance, believed in a fuller understanding of the human being: the tripartite nature of the soul which includes mind, body, *and spirit*. The earlier thinkers maintained that we are truly human because we possess spirit, not just because we think. The offices of rhetoric, which are teaching, moving, and delighting, connect to these three parts of the soul. Specifically, teaching relates to the mind,

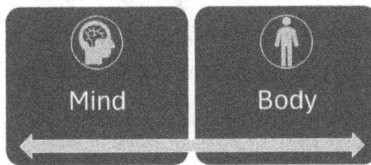

Figure 3.1 Cartesian duality (limited understanding of the human person)

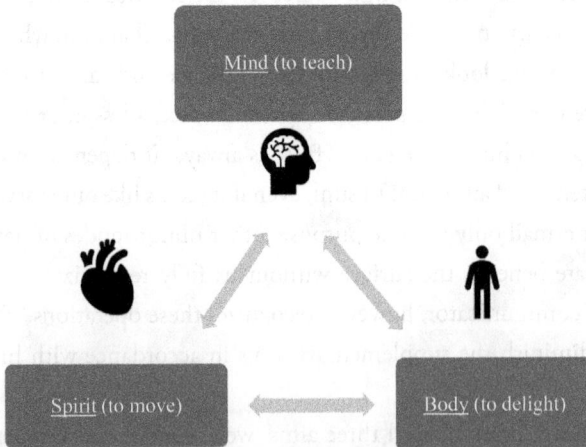

Figure 3.2 Platonic tripartite soul (robust understanding of the human person)

delighting relates to the body, and moving relates to the spirit. These offices engage each of these parts of the human being. We consider this generous understanding of human beings when we consider our audiences in the classical tradition.

Consequently, we don't merely teach and delight; we also inspire and move. Embracing this tripartite understanding, rather than Descartes' cold duality, we more fully command warmth and presence which distinguishes us from mechanical communicators and artificial intelligence. While AI operates through lifeless code and algorithms which are devoid of human spirit, eloquent speakers and writers embrace communication as something beyond mere brains and bodies. Eloquence strives to move and inspire audiences' spirits on a deeper level. Practically speaking, this holistically human (and classical) approach gives the eloquent communicator an edge in the professional sphere. It is an edge because true eloquence is something that generative AI cannot copy. When we embrace our humanity, we embrace an advantage over any type of machine.

Keys to Practical Eloquence

In everything communicated consider the instructive dimension. Instruction is foundational to every piece of communication. Ensure that audiences understand before seeking to persuade. A speaker or writer cannot move someone who does not understand the topic.

In moving our audiences, be nimble. If we overprepare our writing or speech, we are more flexible to alter our course strategically.

The less anxious displays lead to more delightful communication experiences. Again, by preparing our communication beforehand, we can quell our anxiety and hence allow confidence to shine. This radiated confidence leads to more delightful experiences for audiences.

Unite instruction, motivation, and delight into every piece of communication. In doing so, the speech or writing will appeal to the mind, heart, and body. It culminates in fully eloquent experiences.

CHAPTER 4

Canons of Rhetoric

Whether delivering a pitch or writing an e-mail, communication involves a creative process and a creative product. Naturally, we look to expedite and optimize the process so we can deliver a polished product. But the process is not always easy. When writing a report, pitch script, or an even an e-mail, we can find the process daunting. We may sigh and ask ourselves, "Where do I begin?" Luckily, the ancient Greeks and Romans offer a blueprint to follow: a play-by-play of the composition process to ensure that we mix in ingredients of eloquence.

Of the several classical rhetoricians who celebrate this process, Cicero most famously does so in *De Oratore*. Quoting Crassus, an ideal orator, Cicero tells us that good speakers

> ought first to find out what he should say; next, to dispose and arrange his matter, not only in a certain order, but with a sort of power and judgment ; then to clothe and deck his thoughts with language ; then to secure them in his memory ; and, lastly, to deliver them with dignity and grace. (1.31)

In short, he lays out the parts of eloquence or "canons of rhetoric": (1) invention, (2) arrangement, (3) style, (4) memory, and (5) delivery. These five components serve as a perfect checklist when composing eloquent speaking and writing.

Invention: Discover and Connect

For the first part of the process, we should consider the substance of our communication. We figure what we should say. Two dimensions can inform this process: (1) discovery and (2) invention. First, discover evidence in the world that supports a line of reasoning. We may also discover lines of reasoning that have been made elsewhere, perhaps from other thinkers in the past, and evaluate their arguments. Next, we stitch together our own tapestry of reasoning, or "invent" an argument, by considering the relationships between our own truth claims, evidence, and perhaps arguments from the past.

How do we stitch together that initial reasoning? Invention can be understood in a basic three-step process:

1. We "invent" and outline the reasoning of our messages by asking "why" again and again.
2. Then, we weigh whether it is appropriate to share those "why-fueled" reasons with our audience.
3. Finally, for the sake of efficiency, we share some—probably not all—of those reasons.

Asking "why" explores the "because" of each claim. As we discussed in a previous chapter, distilling the "why" is endorsed by business-minded thinkers like Simon Sinek and Elon Musk. The negotiation strategist authors Roger Fisher and William Ury of the classic 1981 book *Getting to Yes*, also discuss "principled negotiation" which adapts this "why-driven" technique to business negotiations. In short, when we ponder principles and causes, we invite deeper thinking and communication.

Let's look at an example chain of this distillation process. I have included underlying assumptions for each claim to hint at the logic that connects each claim to the previous one:

Main thesis to be explored: We should hire another team member.

1. Why should we hire another team member?
   Because our workflow is suffering.
       (Underlying assumption: Hiring more employees should alleviate the suffering workflow.)
2. Why is our workflow is suffering?
   Because our team is stressed out.
       (Underlying assumption: Stress negatively affects workflow.)
3. Why is our team is stressed out?
   Because our team is overworked.
       (Underlying assumption: Overwork causes stress.)

4. Why is our team overworked?

Because our team has too much work to do.

(Underlying assumption: People feel overworked when there's too much work.)

5. Why is there too much work?

Because our company has significantly grown over the last year.

(Underlying assumption: A growing company leads to more work.)

6. Why has our company has significantly grown over the last year?

Because we have taken on more clients.

(Underlying assumption: A company grows because of more clients/revenue.)

7. Why have we taken on more clients?

Because we've been delivering quality service and products to clients.

(Underlying assumption: High-quality services and products attract more clients.)

8. Why have we been delivering quality service and products to clients?

Because we have had a productive workflow up until recently.

(Underlying assumption: A productive workflow leads to high-quality services and products.)

9. Why have we had a productive workflow?

Because we weren't stressed out or overworked.

While we seem to have returned to where we started, the journey still bore fruit. If we are to maintain our past success and maintain our productive workflow, we should probably hire someone. The original thesis-claim stands. We should probably hire another team member.

And when communicating the logic, we can assess each claim as good or bad as we trace each shift. This patient step-by-step process can help when conversing or composing.

Different from invention, discovery still concerns amassing content for our arguments. But we can think of discovery as the gathering of evidence that supports our reasoning. So, in the invention example, perhaps we find similar cases that prove the underlying assumptions that we have made. For example, we say, "productive workflow leads to high quality services and products or evidence." We say that it is true. But is it really true? And how does our audience know that it is true? To communicate that truth, we can find evidence to support that claim. Maybe we uncover case studies about other companies. Maybe, more informally, we share testimony from other business leaders. This evidence serves as proof to increase the probability of truth. It supports the core or fundamental claims that drive our reasoning.

In addition, we can find evidence to prove that particular behavior occurs at *our company*. Again, if we claim that something happens at our company, we should prove it. This proof supports our more *specific* reasoning. It proves that we are not making things up. For example, if we claim that our company has signed more clients. Let's trace that to concrete data about client numbers to support the claim. This way we *say* that it is true. And we *show* that it is true with evidence.

Sometimes we have reasonable intuition that we can eventually find proof (deduction to induction), so we work backward from our claims toward the evidence. Other times we work forward from specific proof to broadband reasoning (induction to deduction). Either way, we want concrete evidence to back up our general claims. And there are several types of evidence to choose. Formally, we can reference concrete evidence like specific studies and numerical statistics. Informally, we can refer to expert testimony, witness testimony, personal anecdotes, or specific examples. We can even use hypotheticals, such as "imagine if" or "what if" scenarios, to help build cases about claims and forecast futures. Of course, hypotheticals should probably not drive our reasoning, but they can add value to arguments. We can find more on hypotheticals and storytelling in Chapter 6.

We can see these types of evidence throughout effective business documents. When we read well-composed shareholder letters, we find them. For example, Warren Buffet's Berkshire Hathway's 2023 shareholder letter is brimming with examples from their past ("During 2023, we did not buy or sell a share of either AMEX or Coke"), hypotheticals ("Would *you* like to be that helpless engineer?"), anecdotes ("Both Charlie and I spent our early years in Omaha public schools ..."), and, of course, numerical data. Without this evidence and support, the letters would fall flat. They would lack clear reasoning and be at least a quarter of the length. In short, they would not exert any eloquence.

Arrangement: Sequence and Flow

Communication unfolds within time. The *positioning* of ideas, rather than only the ideas themselves, can either positively streamline or negatively confuse our audiences. If done well, positioning can motivate audiences to keep listening or reading. If done poorly, it can justify audiences' decisions to walk away. We should always remember that, at any moment during our communication, audiences can stop listening or reading. Nothing requires our audiences to listen to us or read our work. Our audience has freewill. They may not leave the room, but they can certainly zone out. This rhetorical reality calls for vigilance on our part. We want to ensure that our audience never becomes confused or frustrated with our content. We also want to ensure our audience is never left wondering about the relevance of particular information or knowledge in relation to the previous parts.

Ultimately, each section of our communication deserves attention. Specifically, we should consider the sequential arrangement. Organized positioning can provide assurance and control. An organized composition can tame and guide audiences' possible reactions. To this end, effective arrangement minimizes risk of confusion.

Luckily for us, Cicero provides a blueprint of how persuasive speeches unfold; specifically, he refers to legal arguments and judicial speeches for the courts, but his arrangement can still apply to business communication. In *De Oratore*, he explains this blueprint:

> before we enter upon the main subject, the minds of the audience should be conciliated by an *exordium*; next, that the case should be clearly stated; then, that the point in controversy should be established; then, that what we maintain should be supported by proof, and that whatever was said on the other side should be refuted; and that, in the conclusion of our speech, whatever was in our favor should be amplified and enforced, and whatever made for our adversaries should be weakened and invalidated. (1.31)

Ultimately, he proposes six parts of a persuasive speech. Let's break each of these parts down.

1. Exordium (Introduction)

The purpose of the *exordium* is to prepare the audience for the speech, establish the speaker's credibility, and capture the audience's attention. It places the audience in the right "frame of mind" for the forthcoming speech or writing. According to Cicero in *De Inventione*, the *exordium*:

> ought to be sententious to a marked degree and of a high serious-ness, and, to put it generally, should contain everything which contributes to dignity, because the best thing to do is that which especially commends the speaker to his audience. It should con-tain very little brilliance, vivacity, or finish of style, because these give rise to a suspicion of preparation and excessive ingenuity. As a result of this most of all the speech loses conviction and the speaker, authority. (1.18)

He further cautions against some typical faults with *exordiums*, stat-ing that *exordiums* "should not be general, common, interchangeable, tedious, unconnected, out of place, or contrary to the fundamental prin-ciples" (1.18). To revisit the 2023 Berkshire Hathaway shareholder letter, the letter begins with a lengthy acknowledgment of the death of Charlie Munger, "the architect of Berkshire Hathaway." When the shareholder letter officially begins, Warren Buffet emphasizes the savviness of the shareholders and the competitive nature of the markets. In short, Buffet begins with gravity.

The *exordium* is often understood as the "hook." But in a more nu-anced way, it offers more than merely hooking our audience's attention. It stirs a particular "frame of mind." As it does so, it can bolster the author's or speaker's credibility. For example, at the beginning of the 2008 "Let's Rock" Keynote, Steve Jobs begins with: "Good morning. Thank you for coming this morning. We have some really exciting stuff to share with you. Before we do, I wanted to mention this … [gestures to screen]." The slide says: "The reports of my death are greatly exaggerated."

How does this work as an *exordium*? The slide refers to the rumors that Jobs was dying, because, during that year, Jobs lost a lot of weight. Certainly, the joke about his thinning appearance may not have aged well (Note: He received a liver transplant months later and died several years later.). However, by poking fun of rumors of his own death, Jobs emphasizes a type of immortality where audiences think, "Of course, Steve Jobs is not dead. Jobs is never going to die!" In short, the dark humor boosts Jobs' larger-than-life persona.

Before the "reports of my death" slide, of course, he places the audience in an excited state of mind by thanking the audience and mentioning the exciting reveals that will be discussed. He gestures to the purpose of the talk. Whether it is a keynote presentation or a shareholder letter, when we share or remind audiences about the purpose of our communication, we prepare our audience accordingly. But Jobs does more than rationally direct them in his *exordium*. He places viewers in a particular emotional frame of mind. Ultimately, he appeals to his own strong persona and stirs emotion in the few first lines and the first slide. Over the years, Jobs' keynotes regularly offered such creative and persuasive *exordiums*.

2. Narratio (Narration)

The *narratio* provides background information, context, and backdrop necessary for audiences to understand the topic. It outlines the facts of the case or situation, presenting them clearly and concisely. To quote Cicero's *De Inventione*, "the narrative is an exposition of events that have occurred or are supposed to have occurred" (1.19). Directly after his *exordiums*, Steve Jobs often leads audiences through the history of Apple or the history of a previous Apple product toward the beginnings of his Keynote presentations. The history comes before he reveals a new product or new iteration of a product. When he provides this historical context, he offers a *narratio*.

3. Proposito and Partitio (Main Claim and Stance)

These two sections of a composition are quite short. They provide audiences with the thesis and brief reasoning. This part shifts from general topic to specific position, from information into argument. While this classical section often pertains to argumentation, the *proposito* and *partitio* still applies if we are teaching or training others. This early section quickly communicates what subject that our audiences will be specifically learning about.

4. Confirmatio (Confirmation)

The *confirmatio* is the main body of the speech where walk others through deeper reasoning and evidence that supports our *proposito* and *partitio*. This section aims to persuade the audience with strong logical arguments. We unpack the "why" and the "how" in this part of the composition. In this section of Jobs' Keynotes, he explains new product rollouts and how the products work.

5. Refutatio (Refutation)

In this section, we anticipate, outline, and counter opposing arguments. In doing so, we strengthen our position by addressing potential objections and demonstrate the weaknesses in opposing viewpoints—before opposing parties raise the concerns. In Jobs' keynote presentations, he discusses products from Apple's competitors, such as Dell, Microsoft, and Intel. Jobs then explains how Apple products are better than the competitors. When teaching, the *refutatio* introduces naysaying or skeptical perspectives, such as, "Some people may not teach this material because …," and counter them with, "We are learning it because …" The refutation and replies blend dialectical elements into presentations or texts. They offer back-and-forth movement between perspectives that clarify and energize the communication.

6. Peroratio (Conclusion)

The conclusion summarizes the key points of the speech, reinforces the arguments, and makes a final appeal to the audience. It aims to leave lasting impressions and drive the message home, often using emotional appeals. According to Cicero, three elements drive the *peroratio*: a brief summary, amplification to stir the emotions, and a nod to honesty or genuineness.

The *peroratio* briefly summarizes the presentation. But we must be artful with our summary. We don't want to sum things up like we did back in grade school when we wrote five-paragraph essays. In *Rhetorica ad Herennium*, Cicero clarifies that the *peroratio* does not restate the full argument but instead helps "refresh" the audience's memory: "we shall reproduce all the points in the order in which they have been presented, so that the hearer, if he has committed them to memory, is brought back to what he remembers" (2.30). He cautions that the summary must not take audiences back to the *exordium* or *narratio* because it will make the speech seem artificial and fabricated.

The *peroratio* can also stir the emotions. Cicero explains that appeals to pity must be brief because "nothing dries more quickly than a tear" (2.31). But other emotions can work as well, such as anger or excitement. We will discuss the evoking of emotion when addressing pathos in the next chapter. But for now, a quick example will do. In Jobs' keynote presentations, he often did not appeal to pity but to hopeful excitement that comes from making history and marching into the future. For example, in his famous 2007 Keynote on the first iPhone, he ends the presentation reiterating that iPhone adds a major fourth pillar of the company's products—along with Mac, iPod, and Apple TV. He explains that Apple Computer company would then be called Apple Incorporated. By discussing the company name change, audiences feel like they are part of history, which they indeed were. After all, upon launching this new iPhone product, Apple changed the name of the entire company. He seems to fly in the face of Cicero's advice and gesture back to the narration (the history of Apple) from the beginning of the Keynote. He says that the iPhone will change the world much like the Apple computer in 1984 and the iPod in 2001. But he returns to the narration not to summarize his presentation, but to evoke emotion, so he upholds Cicero's advice. Finally, Jobs ends with a quote from hockey player Wayne Gretzky: "I like to skate to where the puck is going to be, not to where it has already been." Jobs proclaims that Apple will continue to do this and innovate into the future. Ultimately, he refreshes the memories of the audience because at the beginning of the presentation, he claims that the iPhone will make history. He fulfills that promise at the end of the presentation when he stirs audience excitement.

Beginnings and Endings

There is a reason why we spend so much time discussing beginnings and endings of our arrangements: Beginnings and endings are absolutely crucial to eloquence. Clearly, Cicero recognized the power of beginnings and endings. But modern user experience (UX) experts do as well. When looking to cognitive science or the cognitive laws of UX, we recognize the same types of principles as the "law of primacy" and the "law of recency." Studies have proven that audiences remember the beginnings of experiences (law of primacy) and the end of experiences (law of recency) much more than the middle of experiences. Therefore, we should embrace these opportunities. Eloquent speaking and writing take Cicero's advice and stir the emotions during these introductory and concluding moments.

We can compound the laws of primacy and recency with a perspective recognized by marketing experts like Robert Cialdini and Seth Godin: people remember emotions over arguments. Therefore, to move audiences, it is persuasive to use emotion at beginning and end. That said, logic is still essential. Logic remains the meat and potatoes of any presentation or piece of writing. However, logic can find a fitting home in the middle of our compositions. While emotion finds its home at the beginning and end.

Style: Plain, Forceful, Middle, and Grand

When we move away from broadband arrangement decisions and zoom closer into the sentence level decisions, we can consider our style. How do we clothe our ideas with language? Do we dress them up? Do we dress them down? Do we have them wear a suit and tie, or a t-shirt and jeans. Do we have them wear board shorts with flip-flops or a polo with kakis and sneakers? Do we have them wear an Adidas tracksuit or army fatigues? Like the stylistic wardrobe decisions of our own lives, the clothing of our ideas depends on appropriateness, context, and how our public will receive it.

Clearly, assorted writing genres guide us toward appropriate writing styles. We can all agree that e-mails are often more informal than business proposals or white papers. We can all agree that text messages are more informal than e-mails. The language and sentencing of e-mails and text messages is less rigid and more casual. But how do we gauge the reception of audiences? When do we ramp up the style of our documents? When do we loosen up the style of our presentations? First, let's look to modern cognitive science. And then we'll look to the ancient wisdom of Cicero.

In his often-cited book *Thinking Fast and Slow*, Daniel Kahneman discusses two types of cognitive schemes—or ways that we think. The first system is System One. System One is fast, automatic, and often subconscious. It includes intuitive reactions and quick judgments. For example, when we instantly recognize a friend's face in a crowd, that's System One at work. It's efficient and useful for everyday tasks but can be prone to errors and biases. The second system is System Two. System Two is slow, deliberate, and conscious. It involves reasoning and critical thinking. When we solve a complex math problem or make a thoughtful decision, we use System Two. System Two is more reliable but requires more effort, energy, and time.

How does these "systems" relate to the style of our diction and sentences? Let's look at two types of styles. For the most part, both passages communicate the same content.

Style A: "This quarter, we have matured as a team."

Style B: "In the evolutionary spirit of our company, we have metamorphized from a crawling organism to a standing upright and dignified creature. We are now ready to roam the wilds as a sustainable unit."

Style A corresponds to Kahneman's System One. It is quick information. We instantly recognize the communicated information. Style B takes longer to understand via the quality (the number of sentences, words, and syllables) as well as the quality (figurative language or "showing" rather than literal language or "telling"). While many business communication handbooks will tell us that Style A is better for business because it is faster and clearer, we shouldn't assume that there is only one way to write for all business contexts. Clearly, most business writing and speaking should apply minimalistic clear style, but sometimes we will need a grander style. And at other times, we will we need to mix the styles.

If eloquence relies on optionality, we should not limit ourselves to one style. After all, the eloquent communicator should not communicate in the same way for every circumstance. The ancient rhetoricians understood this rhetorical flexibility. Let's look at four styles of speaking and writing promoted in the classical era.

Plain Style

People often think that the plain minimalistic style is a modern invention and an American approach. After all, look at American literature, such as the minimalistic style of Ernest Hemingway, Joan Didion, and Cormac McCarthy. Journalistic writing finds itself woven into great modern American literature. Yet minimalistic style did not originate in America. It began in ancient Greece and ancient Rome. It was endorsed by the Atticists or Attics. As a school of thought, the Attics believed that eloquence is found in clarity, not opaqueness. In other words, they were fans of Kahneman's System One.

While Cicero ultimately appreciated more lavish styles, he acknowledged the benefits of plain style because it is the clearest style. Specifically, it works best when teaching because teaching demands clarity. Plain style works best with basic content and informing a public in a direct manner. Augustine appreciated plain style, too. According to Augustine, simple style's advantage is found in its clarity. It conveys information quickly and satisfies audiences' immediate "hunger" for meaning (2.14-15). When do we use plain style? According to Demetrius' *On Style*, plain style properly conveys "simple subjects which are appropriate to it"; as such, it "must consist of current and usual words throughout" (Sect. 190). More complex or heartfelt subjects demand a higher style, which involve more creative expressions and unique diction.

What is the plain style? Specifically, in *Orator*, Cicero describes the user of the style as "restrained and plain" and used by someone who "follows the ordinary usage." (Sect. 76). But this does not mean it is easy to craft.

Cicero goes on to say, "For that plainness of style seems easy to imitate at first thought, but when attempted nothing is more difficult." (Sect. 76). Plain style requires restraint. He explains that the language is "plain and clear; propriety will always be the chief aim. Only one quality will be lacking, ... the charm and richness of figurative ornament" (Sect. 76). The user of plain style "provided he is elegant and finished, will not be bold in coining words, and in metaphor will be modest, sparing in the use of archaisms, and somewhat subdued in using the other embellishments of language and of thought" (Sect. 81). Therefore, some figurative language and humor is allowed but it must be quick and simple. In *Rhetorica ad Herennium*, Cicero finally cautions that our plain style should not fall into "meagre style." "Meagre style" is too austere. It is robotic and lacks humanity. It ignores the "elegant simplicity of diction" and becomes "dry and bloodless" (4.11).

For examples of plain style, we can look to common day-to-day e-mail correspondence. For more official examples, we can return to Buffet's shareholder letters. He uses the plain style. We may think that all shareholder letters use the plain style—and many do. However, some shareholder letters, such as those of Jeff Bezos, seem to approach the "middle style."

Forceful Style

In respect to simple eloquence, Demetrius adds an additional type of plain style, "forceful style." And its overlap with plain style is important to note. Forceful style commands sentence brevity, using "periodic structure[s]" that are "securely knotted at the end" to make sentences "come to a definite stop" (Sect. 244–245). According to Demetrius, these short sentences facilitate a beautiful kind of power (Sect. 252). To this end, brevity becomes forceful in what is *not* being said as well as what *is* being said (Sect. 253). Therefore, in forceful simple style, the negative space between ideas and sentences works rhetorically. The space between periods exerts power. But that said, the flow between these brief sentences is crucial. Naturally, communicators of forceful style must avoid being "jerky" or "course" with their short periodic sentences; after all, they don't want their writing to sound abrasive (Sect. 302–303).

Middle Style

While plain and forceful styles are used primarily to teach or announce, middle style is used to delight. Therefore, if we have an audience who may be a bit more resistant or uninterested, the middle style may be a better fit. Cicero explains that the middle style offers "a minimum of vigour, and a maximum of charm" (26.91). Middle style is "richer than the unadorned style, but plainer than the ornate and opulent style" (26.91). Consequently, the arguments are more developed, more use of metaphors and sustained use of metaphors, and use of wit. In Book I of *De Doctrina Christiana*, Augustine appreciates the middle style because it can "satisfy hunger by means of its plainer passages and remove boredom by means of its obscurer ones" (2.15). As Augustine endorses, middle style strikes a balance between grand and simple styles. Therefore, it strikes a win-win balance for all type of listeners and readers.

How does it work? Cicero explains, it is a "somewhat relaxed" style that has "not descended into the most ordinary prose" (4.9). Middle style relies on fluid movement. It must gracefully alternate between plain and grander styles. To this point, Cicero cautions against "slack style." Slack style neglects the connective tissue when oscillating between plain and grand styles: it "drifts to and fro," "without sinews and joints" (4.11). In contrast to Warren Buffet's shareholder letters, Jeff Bezos' shareholder letters lean toward a middle style of business writing. While the letters may not fully use middle style, its dimensions give us a taste of middle style. The tone is warmer. His sentences lengths and types are more varied. He uses metaphors and memorable lines. Overall, it fosters delight in ways that Buffet does not.

Grand Style

I don't think any shareholder letter is written in the grand style. And it's a good thing too. Grand style is rarely if ever found in business writing. Although eloquent communicators in business should know how to use grand style if particular occasions call for it.

In grand style, according to Cicero, every idea is styled in "the most ornate words that can be found for it, whether literal or figurative"; it implements "smooth and ornate arrangement of impressive words" (4.8).

Demetrius also notes that grand style uses impressive connectives, word-arrangement, figures of speech, and creative diction to illustrate the subject-matter itself (Sect. 38-113). In contrast to minimalism, one might say that grand style leans toward *maximalism*. However, it should not be overdone. Cicero cautions against "swollen style" which tries to be too flowery and uses lofty language that is inappropriate for the occasion (4.10). Like Cicero, Demetrius notes that grand style must be tempered. He suggests that it must not become "frigid" or too "weighty" (Sect. 114). After all, oversophistication can damage a writer's natural connection with his or her audience.

As a Roman orator in the Senate, Cicero celebrated the grand style. In *Orator*, he describes the speaker of grand style as:

> magnificent, opulent stately and ornate; he undoubtedly has the greatest power. This is the man whose brilliance a fluency have caused admiring nations to let eloquence attain the highest power in the state; I mean the kind of eloquence which rushes along with the roar of a mighty stream, which all look up to and admire, and which they despair of attaining. This eloquence has power to sway men's minds and move them in every possible way. … it implants new ideas and uproots the old. (Sect. 97)

Despite such high praise, Cicero offers some words of caution, as well. If we devote all of our energies to this "grand, impetuous and fiery" style and neglect "arrangement, precision, clarity or pleasantry," we will seem "to be a raving madman among the sane, like a drunken reveler in the midst of sober men."—or at the very least, will be annoying and "despised" (Sect. 99). So we should choose our moments for grand style with care.

Most books on business communication ignore grand style. So why should we, as business professionals, care about the grand style? After all, it seems a bit over the top. First, we may find ourselves in formal situations that call for grand style, such as commemorative speeches, eulogies, and tribute speeches. Ceremonial occasions provide appropriate moments to use grand style. Plain style will probably miss the mark when delivering formal speeches.

Furthermore, we need to know grand style to effectively use middle style. And as Cicero suggests, middle style offer the most charm and delight. Additionally, Augustine promotes middle style as the most effective style. In today's attention economy, middle style is both clear and powerful: a perfect hybrid. And remember, middle style toggles between plain and grand styles. Since middle style bounces back and forth between plain and grand styles, *we inevitably need to know grand style to effectively use middle style.* As many great classical rhetoricians tell us, the eloquent communicator knows, implements, and can blend all of three styles, not only plain style.

Memory: Don't Forget

Our technological crutches can interfere with authentic eloquence, if we choose to let them. We undermine our eloquence when we consult our cell phone for information when pitching a potential client. We undermine our eloquence when we use teleprompters during presentations. We undermine our eloquence even when we read our speeches or glance to our notes. While these are common practices nowadays, we may feel that they are acceptable. But keep in mind that eloquence does not consist in doing what is common practice and "good enough." As Socrates explains in Plato's *Crito* (46b-48b): the opinion of the majority is not necessarily the wise position. And we must remember, eloquence offers the wise position. In addition, we have our optics to keep in mind. If we want to be seen as interesting and compelling, we probably don't want to do *only* what's expected of us. We want to *transcend* expectations. After all, the eloquent communicator seeks excellence.

What is the excellent practice according to classical rhetoricians? To showcase the power of our memories. To showcase a breadth of knowledge. To showcase intellectual prowess.

Seem like a tall order? Don't worry. Classical thinkers prescribe some practical methods to do this efficiently and effectively.

Before we get into the methods, let's first consider a question: What type of things should we memorize? In Cicero's *De Oratore*, Crassius explains that we should accurately memorize "as many of our own writings, and those of others, as we can" (1.34). First, we should remember what we have said and written in our past. In addition, we should remember what other people have said and written. And finally, we should refer to these memories in our communication. Naturally, this type of memorization involves remembering things: remembering what we, or others, have said. A broad knowledge about ideas, the world, and history can help with this content: whether we develop that knowledge from formal education, watching documentaries on Netflix, or chatting with wise strangers at the local coffee shop.

Overall, we can explicitly signal our memories with, "As I mentioned in last week's presentation …" or "As Thomas Edison once said …" or perhaps, directly address a partner, "I remember that you once said …." The eloquent communicator weaves these remembered points into the communication. If we integrate past information or knowledge into our present speaking or writing, we texture our speech or writing. We emphasize that we are part of an ongoing conversation. It connects us to a stream of wisdom, which, as mentioned in the Introduction chapter, offers a powerful dimension of eloquence.

But content is not the only dimension to memorize. According to Cicero's Crassus, we may want to memorize rhetorical and persuasive moves, as well (1.34). Therefore, in addition to content, we can memorize tactics discussed in rhetorical handbooks such as Aristotle's *Rhetoric*, Cicero's *De Oratore*, Quintilian's *Institutio Oratoria*, and even this book (if I may be so bold). We can memorize them for eventually use. But more effectively, we can inscribe them onto our habits, which is a deeper kind of memorization. Of course, habit-building takes practice and repetition.

Thomas Aquinas, Cicero, and Quintilian offer ways to help us remember effectively. In his commentary on Aristotle's *On Memory*, Aquinas prescribes a basic process of memorization. It may seem simple—but, still, it is important.

1. First, we should set in order what we want to remember.
2. Second, we should apply the mind deeply to it.
3. Third, we should think it over often.
4. Fourth, when we want to recollect it, we should take the chain of connections by one end, which will bring the rest with it. (452a2)

The first three steps are clear. We recognize what we want to memorize, think about it deeply (the qualitative dimension), and think about it often (the quantitative dimension). But what is he saying in this last step? Emphasizing Aristotle's theory of memory, Aquinas tells us that we remember more effectively when we think in associative ways. We remember better when we connect abstract ideas to concrete images. Let's say that we want to remember a compelling idea from a documentary that we watched 2 years ago. Rather than trying to remember the idea outright, we can begin by remembering *where* we watched the documentary. Perhaps we watched it in the living room of our apartment with our friend Marie. Once we recreate the experience in our mind's eye, we may then recall superficial parts of the documentary that are easier to remember, perhaps, some images or soundbites. Finally, we connect these images and memories to our goal: remembering the sought after compelling idea. Ultimately, the comfortable buildup serves as a graceful bridge into more difficult memories. We can remember "around something" as a means to more accurately remember the pursued memory.

What if we must deliver a speech? Should we memorize it? Yes. Maybe not word for word, but ancient rhetors promote the memorization of speeches. Classical orators didn't read presentations or use teleprompters for speeches. While today, many people read their presentations from slides, or even read presentations from paper, this practice is not compelling. Reading to others wastes an opportunity to naturally connect with our audience. It weakens the energy of our delivery. It casts doubts about our own intellectual proficiency. And it casts doubts on if we composed the speech. After all, if we read a speech, we could merely be reading someone else's words.

So how can we memorize our own speeches? In *Rhetorica ad Herennium*, Cicero tells us that we remember images, symbols, and concrete details much better than words and abstract ideas (3.16-21). Therefore, he offers a way to use images—specifically through location-based imagery—to guide our speech. He and Quintilian offer the *loci* of memory (*De Oratore* 2.86-88; *Institutio Oratoria* 11.2.17-26). According to them, we can break up our speech into divisions and subdivisions and connect those division and subdivisions to rooms within an imaginary mansion. As we move through our speech, we allow our imaginations to guide us through the mansion room by room. We connect each room with parts of the talk. Therefore, the hook may be the front yard, the introduction may be the foyer, the context/history section of our speech becomes the hallway, the middle part of the speech may be the living room, and the conclusion may be found in the back kitchen. When we associate ideas with concrete places, even if they are made up, we remember them better. In addition, we can even envision items in each room that connect to details from sections of our speech. For instance, we may remember the happy takeaway at the end of our talk by imaginatively recalling a chocolate cake that rests on the counter of the kitchen, the last room of our "house of memory."

While we may not use this *loci* approach to remember our speech on the fly, it can still help us prepare for our speech. The rooms and images help ideas stick in our brain. So even as we rehearse, we can play with the *loci* approach and engage our imagination to memorize our arguments and arrange our ideas.

Delivery: Charm, Convince, and Close

In *Institutio Oratoria*, Quintilian shares that Greek orator Demosthenes famously proclaimed "delivery" as the most important element of eloquence: "not merely the principle [of delivery], but the only excellence" (11.3.6). Both Quintilian and Cicero share Demosthenes' point because they agree with him. In *Institutio Oratoria*, Quintilian spends thousands of words on how to deliver speeches well. Cicero appreciated delivery, too. Cicero remarked that delivery is the "sole and supreme power in oratory; without it, a speaker of the highest mental capacity can be held in no esteem; while one of moderate abilities, with this qualification, may surpass even those of the highest talent" (3.56). Demosthenes, Quintilian, and Cicero still appear to be correct. And their advice aligns with modern studies. According to recent studies, body language and verbal delivery account for 63 to 90 percent of the impression that we leave on our audience. So, with verbal communication, how we say something is just as important, perhaps even *more* important, than what we say.

Our body language matters. Therefore, as is best practice in modern TED talks, we shouldn't obscure our bodies with objects such as a podium, table, or laptop. This way, nothing blocks our delivery from our audience. And we can use our bodies to communicate more fully. In *De Oratore*, Cicero explains that our gestures should match the emotions communicated: "not the gesture of the stage, expressive of mere words, but one showing the whole force and meaning of a passage, not by gesticulation but by emphatic delivery" (3.59). The message should be announced through a strong "exertion of the lungs," not the artificial delivery used by actors in the theater but instead delivery used in the sporting arena (3.59). In other words, our delivery should be confident and sincere. Several parts of the body can be used when delivering speech. Regarding the specifics of powerful delivery, Cicero remarks that "the arm should be considerably extended, as one of the weapons of oratory; the stamping of the foot should be used only in the most vehement efforts, at their commencement or conclusion" (3.59). He remarks that even "the eyes bear sovereign sway" (3.59). So, we should consider our eyes as well as our arms and legs. That is, we should think about where (and how) we look when we speak. But rhetorically, Cicero recognizes that delivery should depend on the circumstance, the audience, the speech, and the speaker's countenance. In short, we should consider how we use our entire body to communicate our message clearly and emphatically.

But of course, Cicero emphasizes powerful style, as did many classical rhetoricians of the time. While these rhetoricians admit that gentility can have a place in speeches, they seem less concerned with discussing "warm" deliveries. This effort is taken up more fully by modern charisma coaches such as Vanessa Van Edwards and Olivia Cabane. Van Edwards and Cabane point out that warmth plays a crucial part of charismatic delivery. Therefore, we should consider a warm delivery in addition to a powerful delivery. The difference between the two is clear. While powerful delivery is found in actions like backward leans, eye contact when speaking, serious expressions, longer speech duration, faster speech rate, louder volume, and directive gestures (like finger-pointing and head shaking), warmth is found in forward leans, eye contact when listening, happy expressions, shorter speech durations, slower speech rate, softer volume, and accepting gestures (like head-nodding and shoulder dropping). Which one do we use? It depends on what we are comfortable with and the situation and audience. And we can always mix-and-match, so we get the best of both worlds: warm power or powerful warmth.

In her 2012 book *The Charisma Myth*, Olivia Cabane explains that charismatic personalities are not merely natural gifts. Rather, charisma can be developed through practice. According to Cabane, presence is an important dimension of radiating charisma. And she insists that it can be learned. Charismatic speakers (and I would add writers as well) reveal that they are present with listeners or readers. Presence can be evidenced through a series of signals, such as eye contact, body language, nodding, asking questions, not thinking about what we want to say next, not glancing around the room, and not looking to our cell phone or watch. Being present in the moment with others radiates warmth. According to Cabane, warmth is the cozy feeling when connecting with another human being: when ideas flow, when understanding is shared, and when passion is mutual. Even if two communicators do not agree on a particular ideology or worldview, warmth can still unfold via presence. Presence, on behalf of both parties, becomes essential to crafting warm and likeable communication experiences.

Eloquent delivery embraces the present moment and facilitates presence. The more presence is woven into the interaction, the more audiences are "with us" in the interaction. Presence optimizes the connectivity of our communication and the warmth of the human-to-human interaction. Think about it. We often bond and connect over shared experience. It can be a reason why strangers connect so strongly and quickly in times of crisis.

For example, I was once stuck in a small one-gate airport in Dickinson, North Dakota, seeking to fly back home to Fort Myers, Florida. We had boarded the plane, but it started to snow, and we weren't able to take off. After we flew back into airport from the canceled flight, we were told that the storm would last all day. Sitting disappointed in the airport, I overheard that a couple was going to drive 7 hours through the snow to Colorado to catch their flight in Denver. They were looking for volunteers to join the car ride. The weight of passengers would help the car handle better in the snow. I rolled the dice. Along with two other strangers, I volunteered to join them. Over the next 7 hours, the five of us bonded, talking with one another and sharing points of view as five people from different regions and cultures. I still look back at those 7 hours and I feel warm and cozy. It was like we became a family in a relatively short amount of time. The crisis orchestrated a deep presence. It connected us all in a lasting way.

We have all had crises where we bonded with other people through a shared moment. While we don't need a crisis to do this, we can facilitate presence by connecting our audience through well-delivered communication experiences. And this involves being warm and present with others so that they can be warm and present with us.

Keys to Practical Eloquence

In constructing arguments and content, ask "why" repeatedly. It can help construct profound and lasting content.

Thoughtfully consider the arrangement of speeches and texts. In doing so, emotional modes of persuasion may be placed toward beginnings and ends of audiences' experiences; the reasoning can be placed in the middle of audiences' experiences.

Keep in mind: There is not only one style of language for professional communication. Think beyond the typical advice found in modern business communication handbooks. Specifically, consider forced, middle, and grand styles in addition to the typical plain style.

Memorization is essential to eloquence. While memorization is often overlooked in today's age of technology, look to flex the memory and showcase connections to the past. Explicit recollection can wow audiences as well as facilitate greater understanding.

When writing, conversing, or delivering presentations, seek warmth, power, and presence. It transports audiences into dynamic and delightful communication experiences.

CHAPTER 5

Active Persuasion: Ethos, Pathos, and Logos

Arguably Aristotle's three persuasive appeals the probably the most well-known contributions from his handbook *Rhetoric*. When students learn rhetoric in first-year writing courses at many of today's universities, students briefly learn about these appeals. Sadly, that's often where the classical rhetoric instruction ends. In this chapter, we will double-click on these appeals so that we can optimize them in our professional communication.

With Aristotle's persuasive appeals, the communicator emphasizes three dimensions of the communication for persuasive effect. The three dimensions are:

1. Speaker or writer
2. Audience
3. Reality shared by audience and the communicator

When we emphasize our character as speaker or writer, we appeal to ethos. When we emphasize the frame of mind of the audience, we appeal to pathos. When we emphasize the reality or proof of the argument, we appeal to logos. These three elements combine within any given composition—in different proportions—to form an eloquent and persuasive whole.

Again, while the *officia oratoris* (see Chapter 3) and the canons of rhetoric (see Chapter 4) are arguably more crucial in communication, these three appeals are the most commonly known elements of persuasion. For decades, they have frequented communication guides and college textbooks. *Harvard Business Review* articles, like Carmine Gallo's "The Art of Persuasion Hasn't Changed in 2,000 Years," discuss them. Business writing books, like Paul MacRae's *Business and Professional Writing: A Basic Guide for Americans*, discuss them. Books on UX, like Edward Stull's *UX Fundamentals for Non-UX Professionals*, discuss them.

While Aristotle may be briefly mentioned in these business-minded texts, the books do not explore the nuances of Aristotle's concepts. Moreover, the texts seldom mention ancient rhetoricians apart from Aristotle. In short, modern business books seldom deeply dive into the components of ethos, pathos, and logos. This chapter will provide those deeper looks.

Ethos: Foster Trust

It is fitting to discuss ethos first because it is so foundational to get someone to listen to or read our work. Ethos concerns the character and likability of the speaker or writer. To be persuasive and eloquent, we want to communicate trustworthiness so that our audience believes in us, and, by extension, believes what we say or write. This foundation can be vital to the beginning of any message, especially if the audience does not know us.

Ethos pivots upon trust. The professional world is filled with articles about the importance of trust in the workplace. Any manager should recognize that trust is paramount. In his 2017 *HBR* article, Paul A. Zak traces how workplace trust-building is an issue of neuroscience. When we nourish trust through our management style, our team feels good which makes them more productive. We can extend this insight to communication. If we nurture trust in our communication, we make audiences feel good. This helps them understand our message more clearly—and want to understand our message. Consequently, it guides them to be better listeners and readers. It elevates our persuasive potential. However, trust is delicate to maintain and catastrophic if betrayed. It is hard to build, but easy to destroy. A breach of trust is hard to bounce back from. As Galford and Anne Seibold Drapeau observe in their 2003 *HBR* article, "Enemies of Trust,": "If people think the organization acted in bad faith, they'll rarely forgive—and they'll never forget." So we should take trust seriously.

In Book Two of his *Rhetoric*, Aristotle explains three elements that "inspire confidence in the orator's own character": good sense (or practical wisdom), goodwill, and good moral character (or virtue). Consequently, these three dimensions help audience's trust us. Like many of Aristotle's constructions, these three are interconnected to one another. Each informs the other. Therefore, to eloquently appeal to ethos, we should see to balance all three dimensions because each makes the others stronger.

1. Good sense

First, when appealing to character, we should ensure good sense or practical wisdom. We want to radiate common-sense that help to get things done. This may be obvious in the professional world, but practical wisdom is crucial when building trust with audiences.

There are two ways to miss the mark with common sense. If audiences perceive that we don't know what we are talking about, they will stop listening to us and stop reading our work. This is an obvious point. After all, we wouldn't trust Timmy, the 4-year-old from down the block, if he was to advise us about the finance strategy of our company. Any 4-year-old wouldn't have the knowledge or experience to offer sound advice. We wouldn't take him seriously. But while quantity of knowledge matters, the quality of knowledge also matters. Accordingly, our character may suffer if we do not convey *actionable* knowledge. In other words, our audiences may believe that we know a lot, but it doesn't end there. They need to know that our knowledge is practical. Without practical knowledge, we may also lose our listener or reader.

For example, I've spoken with several hiring managers outside of academia who confess that when they see a candidate with a PhD on the pile of resumes, they throw the resume in the trash. Why? From the manager's experience, PhD candidates are often too abstract and theoretical. They fail to communicate practically. They speak like they are in a classroom, not working in a business.

This frustration is not merely a modern trend. It goes back to classical times.

Despite being a lover of philosophy, Cicero admits in *De Oratore* that speakers should sometimes leave philosophical talk behind and evoke emotions in a practical manner. Sometimes an orator should save lofty philosophical references for times of quiet retirement because philosophical references can utterly contrast "ordinary life and social manners" of audience members (1.52). In other words, sometimes we should abandon bookishness and communicate so we can get things done. It is fine to be smart, but when we communicate in the workplace, we want to communicate practical wisdom. This practicality fosters trust and magnetism with our audience.

An easy way to communicate practical takeaways was already explored in a previous chapter. Specifically, we can consider our audience's desire to understand "What is in it for me?" or "How does this benefit me?" If we patiently and clearly explain how our message improves our listener or reader's life, they will be captivated. To them, we will have "good sense." We will radiate a strong practical ethos. Audiences will appreciate the knowledge because we have just made their lives easier.

2. Goodwill

Secondly, we should radiate goodwill. We should show our audiences that we care about their well-being, growth, and success. Again, if we establish goodwill at the beginning of a presentation, e-mail, or conversation, audiences can trust us throughout the experience. While some professionals may roll their eyes at colleagues who begin e-mails with "I hope you had a good weekend!" or "Happy Friday!" these opening lines can evoke positive emotion and establish goodwill. While some people may see such introductions as empty timewasters, the lines contribute to an e-mail's eloquence. They demonstrate that we care about our colleague. Specifically personal opening lines may feel less hollow, such as, "I hope you had a good time up north this weekend!" or "Congrats again on securing Friday's deal." Because these remarks show that we remember something specific about our reader, they indicate that we appreciate him or her. They build a connection.

Now, of course, we should smartly read the moment. If we should directly get to business, then by all means, we should not waste room and time with statements of goodwill. Moreover, if goodwill is already established (e.g., perhaps we have recently built rapport with a colleague in the hallway 3 minutes before sending an e-mail), we obviously do not have to emphasize goodwill. Furthermore, if a deal requires more formality or if our reader is a stoic individual, we should tread lightly with the enthusiasm of our goodwill.

We can once again consider audiences' "What is in it for me" desires when kindling goodwill. When we clearly share practical takeaways in our communication, we establish good sense and goodwill. After all, when we share practical advice, we demonstrate that we care about improving the lives of our listeners or readers. Practical advice is a gift to the other person. We are not stingily hoarding advice, but we share it with our partner in a giving manner. This communicates goodwill. So, when appealing to ethos, we should remember to share takeaways but also ensure that our audience understands how our message, information, or wisdom benefits them.

3. Good moral character

Finally, we cultivate trust by being a good person. Are the claims proposed in our communication ethical? Do we adhere to the ethics of the organization or company? Outside of our specific communication, do we live an ethical life?

While ethical nuances may differ because of different priorities and missions of businesses and communities, the ancient world offered some broadband concepts that may be useful when framing virtue—and bolstering appeals to ethos. The ancient world was more serious than today's world. The eloquent speaker was not someone who merely spoke well, but rather, as Quintilian tells us, a speaker "cannot speak well unless he be a good man" (2.25.24). Obviously, we don't want to "virtue signal" our goodness too heavily because an audience may see it as showboating. Or they may think that we are flaunting that we are better than they are. Or maybe even worse, they may sense that we are guilting them into changing their ways. In other words, if we emphasize morality too much or too explicitly in the workplace, we may come across as insecure which hurts our appeal to ethos, rather than strengthening it.

The ancient rhetoricians recognized that a natural way to express morality is to live a moral life. Professionally, we can do this by treating our team with respect or taking our company's mission seriously. We build a positive reputation. Audiences hear about that reputation—and then we do not have to draw attention to it. Our ethos is strengthened as a by-product. Audiences will begin to see and hear that we are decent people, how we ethically manage our team, or how we take our company's mission seriously. Consequently, they trust us more.

Some important ancient virtues to consider are as follows:

Virtue #1: Temperance

Alongside prudence, temperance is an important classical virtue. While many classical thinkers recognized its importance, Aristotle most famously illustrated it in his *Nicomachean Ethics*. He explained that extremes are problematic. On the one hand, there is excess; on the other hand, there is deficiency. Much like Goldilocks and the "three little bears," the middle ground is often the best route. To use an illustration from Aristotle, to rush into battle is rash, to run away from battle is cowardice, but to stand one's ground and fight is courageous (1116a5-8). Therefore, if we argue for a moderate position rather than extreme perspectives, our communicated ethos can be strengthened. We can appear more thoughtful and controlled because moderation rationally recognizes a win-win position between two extreme positions.

Temperance can also be demonstrated through temperate communication itself. If our speaking or writing is tempered, we are seen as temperate by association. Perhaps we may use assertive word choices rather than aggressive word choices or passive word choices. Perhaps we use middle or plain style rather than grand style. Perhaps we vary our sentence lengths rather than use only lengthy or short sentences. All of these options display moderation not only in what we say but *how* we say it. Both the style and substance of our communication can signal that we are moderate people.

Virtue #2: Fortitude and Courage

Sometimes it may take fortitude to remain patient and silent. Our silence can communicate to others. For instance, if we are on a committee and everyone is becoming fiery and outraged, we can keep our cool. Our silence serves our ethos. It signals that we are more controlled and thoughtful. And then when we choose to speak or write, people may listen or read with more interest. We bear our emotion until a precise moment in time, or what the ancient Greeks called *kairos*, when we should communicate it.

While sometimes we should remain silent, other times we should courageously speak up or write. We are courageous when we discern the opportune moment or *kairos* and then vulnerably interact with a public. Therefore, sometimes it takes fortitude to remain silent, and other times it takes courage to speak up. In both situations, we should assess the situation and find that well-placed moment to courageously speak or write. And when we do, our message can pack a lot of power.

Virtue #3: Gravitas

Gravitas can be defined as seriousness. More specifically, it recognizes the grave importance of ideas that should be taken seriously. While seriousness may not be considered a virtue in the modern world, the virtue of gravitas pervaded ancient Roman thought and culture. Cicero notably discussed gravitas in Book One of *De Officiis*. He argued that a ruler should command a serious demeanor and embrace the role of responsibility. He further discussed how public officers must conduct themselves with dignity, virtue, and seriousness to fulfill their duties effectively (1.93).

Schools of Stoicism probably most famously endorsed the virtue of gravitas. Roman Stoic ruler Marcus Aurelius explains that people should aspire for "gravity without airs" in his *Meditations*. This phrase captures the Stoic ideal of maintaining a serious, dignified demeanor without frills or arrogance. It suggests that a natural weightiness of character comes from inner strength and self-awareness rather than external posturing. Accordingly, Marcus Aurelius and other Stoics, like Epictetus and Seneca, privileged philosophy: the inner life over individual passions. By emphasizing reason and virtue over fleeting desires or impulses, Stoics aimed toward states of composure and moral decency that depends upon gravitas. Furthermore, Stoics emphasized contemplation of one's moment of death or *momento mori*, which serves as a powerful tool for cultivating gravitas. Regular reflection on life's finitude helps foster humility and develop a sense of urgency in living virtuously. But for rhetorical purposes, *momento mori* can aid business communication by helping us recognize urgency and the value of time. It helps us not waste our listener's or reader's time. Therefore, gravitas helps us take our communication seriously. Gravitas helps us get down to business, stay on task, and make every word and sentence do something so that we don't waste time.

Virtue #4: *Dignitas*

Dignitas is a Latin word that resists direct English translation. It doesn't directly translate to mere "respect." Some modern interpreters appropriate this word to mean the duty of Romans to their cultural stations. While this duty played a role, the more accurate meaning of *dignitas* concerns human honor and dignity. So, *dignitas* transcends mere social functionality, but, like all classical virtues, it connects to a philosophical or contemplative meaning.

Specifically, *dignitas* does not sink down to a lower or mediocre level. It opposes the modern "good enough" attitude. It doesn't look to make everyone feel OK but raises others toward honorable human excellence. For someone to extend *dignitas* outward toward others, they signal that they have confidence in other people's abilities. This confidence is persuasive. In the spirit of *dignitas*, we would communicate in ways that inspire upward betterment because we respect our audiences' human potential. While many modern companies and schools may lower the bar to make employees and students feel good, classical ethics promotes a different priority. *Dignitas* sets the bar high. While the goal may be harder to achieve, *dignitas* makes teams feel strong when they finally reach that high level. Consequently, *dignitas* helps others fulfill their potential rather than compromising it.

4. Candor

While Aristotle discusses three elements to bolster our appeals to ethos, we can add a fourth element: candor. Like the other three, candor still plays an important role in business communication today. In her 2017 book *Radical Candor*, former Apple and Google executive Kim Scott explains her concept of "radical candor." She defines "radical candor" as personal caring for other people and the company—while at the same time, directly challenging people and the company. This *both/and* approach helps managers balance the sweet spot for meaningful feedback: one that is not overly harsh and not insincere. From a company culture standpoint, Scott's radical candor fosters an environment where employees safely express their thoughts and concerns, which leads to better performance and stronger teamwork. However, candor did not merely come onto the scene in 2017. In the earlier 2009 *HBR* article "A Culture of Candor," James O'Toole and Warren G. Bennis argue that companies foster a culture of candor to innovate, respond to stakeholders' needs, and operate efficiently. The authors emphasize the need for transparent communication within organizations. From their perspective, leaders should admit errors, encourage employees to speak truthfully, and reward those who sincerely challenge the status quo. They maintain that such transparency helps organizations remain economically, ethically, and socially sustainable.

Candor remains essential in modern management. And it extends back to the classical era. Speaking or writing with candor appeals to ethos. Plato explores this topic in several dialogues—but probably most prominently in *Gorgias*. In *Gorgias*, he defines strong ethos a bit differently from Aristotle. Plato characterizes ethos as knowing wisdom, caring for the listener, and being willing to tell the truth (487a). The willingness to tell the truth is candor. Through the character of Socrates, Plato goes on to distinguish truth-telling from other types of communication, such as flattery. He explains that the honest communicator does not aim at gratification or what is most pleasant; instead, the honest communicator aims at what is *best* (521d6-e1). To illustrate this, he contrasts pastry baking with medicine (464a-465e). Pastries excite the appetites by tasting good, while medicine heals the soul and tastes bitter. These differences are not mutually exclusive. Much like flavorful children medicine today, we can sweeten the bitter medicine to make it taste palatable or even delightful. To quote the wisdom of Mary Poppins: "a spoonful of sugar helps the medicine go down." And we can do it in ways that do not compromise the healing power or truth. The eloquent professional communicator possesses both candor (healing medicine) and delightful likability (sweetness). They express a truthful "treatment" that works best for business while, if they can, make treatment taste like "pastry."

Pathos: Share a Frame of Mind

According to marketers, emotion is extremely powerful. Customers are seduced by advertisements and remain loyal to companies because the marketing sustain customers' emotional wants. On a more interpersonal level, successful salespeople often make their customers feel well liked, which, again, communicates a persuasively positive emotional charge. So, why is there so much emphasis on emotion? Although it may seem like a strange phenomenon, people often believe emotion over logical arguments. For example, Robert Cialdini shares a sociological experiment where a group of people did not believe scientists' arguments about Darwinian evolutionary theory until the likeable actor George Clooney advocated the theory. The group believed the friendly actor over the authoritative scientists. The same experiment was repeated with actor Emma Watson. Again, the population believed likeability over credibility. Why? Because likeability makes people feel better.

This importance of emotion is not a new phenomenon. Ancient Roman rhetorician Quintilian explains, emotion is a "supreme" element in eloquence: "Proofs in our favor, it is true, may make the judge think our cause the better, but impressions on his feelings make him wish it to be the better, and what he wishes he also believes" (6.2.5). He continues to say that as soon as the judge becomes angry, feels pity, or leans favorably, he or she begins to take a personal interest in the case. And this can possess persuasive power.

This tension between emotional and rational sides of our brain is analogized by NYU psychologist Jonathan Haidt in his 2006 book *The Happiness Hypothesis: Finding Modern Truth in Ancient Wisdom* and is referenced in Chip Heath and Dan Heath's 2010 book *Switch: How to Change Things When Change Is Hard*. Both books explain our emotional side as a massive elephant and our rational side as the rider of the elephant. While the elephant is a force to be reckoned with, we must control that force with rational discipline and strength.

While it is a good analogy, both books merely lifted the analogy from Plato's *Phaedrus* dialogue. And in doing so, Haidt and the Heaths reduced the original tripartite framework into a basic duality. Plato's classical psychology is more intricate. Consequently, it can give our eloquence more direction. In Plato's *Phaedrus*, the character of Socrates does not illustrate an elephant rider but a charioteer who controls two winged horses: a good horse and a wild horse (245c-249d). The good horse represents the spirit that leads us to goodness, and the bad horse represents our appetites that lead us toward unruly earthly passions. The winged horses must be balanced and harmonized by the rational charioteer for the chariot to go forward—and optimally, upward—in a purposeful way. While Haidt and the Heaths' elephant analogy may be easier to understand, Plato's charioteer more accurately represents the complexity of our emotions and passions. As eloquent communicators, not only do we teach others how to tame their wild horses, but we can persuade them to cultivate the good parts of themselves. Ultimately, Plato's complex charioteer offers a more constructive analogy than the elephant rider.

Centuries earlier in his *Rhetoric*, Aristotle cautions communicators against emotional capacity, saying that emotion can warp the ruler of a carpenter (1354a24-26). Emotions can bias argument. Emotions can bias our audience before they hear our arguments. They can be unethically used to manipulate audiences rather than sway them with eloquence. According to Aristotle, emotions sway people's judgments because they are charged with pain or pleasure (1378a20-23). To use emotions persuasively we should consider three important aspects: (1) the makeup of a particular emotional state of mind, (2) who our audience may feel the emotion toward, and (3) why they may feel the emotion (1378a23-26). Aristotle explains that we need to know all three dimensions. If we know only one or two, it is not enough (1378a27).

For example, let's assume that a manager named Ben wants to calm his team in a moment of crisis. First, he should recognize the frame of mind that generally makes people feel calm. Then he should determine the type of person whom their team may feel calm toward. Finally, Ben should strategize how to stir that emotion in his team.

For the first stage, Ben recognizes that calmness is the opposite of anger or anxiety. For the second stage, he recognizes that people express calmness toward humble people whom they respect. Ben realizes that people become calm when others show goodwill toward them. Consequently, as a manager, he can facilitate calmness through a secure and successful environment—and by evoking satisfaction. In short, Ben must

know what calmness is, how to model calmness as a leader, and identify the appropriate communication and conditions that evoke calmness. According to Aristotle, "laughing and feasting" evoke calm feelings
(1380b1-4). Ben decides to do just that. He tells a couple of jokes, so the
team laughs. Then he orders some pizza for the team so they can "feast"
and feel satisfied. Still today, Aristotle's advice holds true. Both laughing
and eating put people at ease.

How Do We Evoke Emotion?

As discussed in "Arrangement: Sequence and Flow" section of Chapter 4,
we can influence audiences' frames of mind at the beginnings of compositions, conversations, or presentations. As Cicero discusses, *exordiums*
can initially move the will so that audiences want to learn and pay attention. We all tend to remember beginning parts and concluding parts
of experiences more vividly than the middle of experiences. Moreover,
as Robert Cialdini and Seth Godin tells us, people remember how encounters feel more than they remember minutia of arguments. Therefore,
when considering the persuasive use of emotions, we may want to evoke
them at the beginning and end of speeches or documents. The introduction and concluding emotions do not have to be mutual exclusive.
We can kindle sustained emotions between both parts. This approach
is seen in Steve Jobs' keynote presentations where he rouses excitement
before and after he discusses Apple product rollouts. Using beginning and
end placements, we can also evolve the emotion as long as the evolution
makes sense. For example, at the beginning of a presentation, we may
calm audiences about a crisis, and then by the end of presentation, evoke
excitement for the future of the company. The emotions appropriately
progress. Calmness can naturally progress toward hope.

Riffing off Cicero, Quintilian explains that speakers—and I would
add, writers—must actually feel the emotions and passions that they want
to stir in their audiences (6.2.25-28). We shouldn't try to fake it. Our
audience can feel the difference. They can detect falsehood. In *Institutio
Oratoria*, Quintilian confesses that in some speeches, he literally moved
himself to tears when communicating (6.2.36). And the visible tears offer
powerful evidence that an argument indeed deserves pity. After all, to put

it simply, if we don't feel the emotion, why should the audience feel it? As Horace says, "Before you can move me to tears, you must grieve yourself … Sad words are required by a sorrowful face; threats come from one that is angry, jokes from one that is jolly, serious words from the solemn." Furthermore, "when a person smiles, people's faces smile in return." In other words, we imitate feelings of other human beings. It is part of our biological tendency to mirror and imitate others. Therefore, as Horace claims in his *Ars Poetica*, poems should do more than merely attract others; they should lead audience's emotions in a particular direction. So, in the professions, it is not enough for us to build aesthetically pleasing presentation slides or to craft well-proportioned sentences. To be eloquent, we must stir the emotions to sway the listener or reader. As Cicero tells us, "to sway is victory; for it is the one thing of all that avails most in winning verdicts" (Sect. 69).

While an emotional delivery is important, poetic style can certainly help stir the emotion too. As already discussed, metaphors and similes help dazzle audiences and excite their imaginations and emotions. For example, a manager named Beth, looking to motivate her team, says, "We need to get past this obstacle with determination." Does this statement engage the emotions? Not really. Even if Beth delivers the words with vim and vigor, the statement still probably wouldn't fire up her team. The words need some work. So, to more effectively stir the emotions with the language, Beth may want to say something like, "We need to scale this mountain with fire in our bellies and dirt under our fingernails." Although a bit over-the-top, the style is exciting, imaginative, memorable, and motivational. Clearly, grand and middle styles play an active role when engage the emotions in this way.

Stirring the emotions is an active method. Consequently, it involves presence. By evoking images of "mountains" and "fingernails," audiences become present with the content, and present with the communicators. This shared moment helps stir emotions. Aristotle uses the Greek word for "stir" when discussing persuasive emotions because emotions are indeed in flux. Emotions involve movement. And such activity helps move our audiences' will. Therefore, strong action words, that is, powerful verbs, are paramount when moving others' emotions. After all, verbs literally communicate *movement*. So, we should embrace strong specific verbs in our speech or writing when stirring audiences' feelings.

In the previous example, Beth's specific verb to "scale" replaces the boring action to "go past." After all, "go past" is not specific. The verb does not evoke an image. In contrast, "scale" is more vivid. Therefore, it offers a more excitement. The verb radiates more energy. It engages the imagination. That said, Beth may add *even more* action to the mountain metaphor to incite even more energy. Revising for action, the sentence, "We need to scale this mountain with fire in our bellies and dirt under our fingernails." can read: "We need to scale this mountain with fire *blazing* in our bellies and dirt *caked* under our fingernails." The revision adds the words "blazing" and "caked" so that the statement radiates even more movement. The fires are "blazing"—and even the stagnant noun "dirt" now does something in the sentence. It is "caked." Ultimately, with appeals to pathos in mind, we should pay close attention to our diction. Changing words here and there, specifically verbs, can make significant impacts.

Logos: Sell a Stable Reality

When we appeal to logos, we gesture to the argument itself and its proof: both of which orient audiences toward reality outside of themselves. Now every piece of communication involves argument: a stance and reasoning why something is true or probable. The reasoning can be implied; or the reasoning can be more explicit. For example, we can say to a coworker: "Marie is a great salesperson." And a coworker may agree, and the conversation may move on to another topic. We have supplied a claim about Marie, but we did not share any reasoning. If we say "Marie is a great salesperson. She is so passionate." We have now shared our reasoning—specifically, "Marie is a great salesperson *because* she is so passionate." We have supplied an explicit argument. If we feel the need, we can further develop the logic. As a third possibility, we can say, "Marie is a great salesperson. She is so passionate. I've seen her in action several times and she closes deals every time!" Again, the argument is explicit but now we offer proof. In short, explicit arguments appeal to logos much more than solitary claims. In the third iteration, we appeal to logos even more. The expanded evidence draws the audience's attention more to the proof. The more that we direct attention and spend time with the logic and proof of arguments, the more we appeal to logos.

How to we make these logos-centric decisions? First, let's unpack the word "argument." The terms "argument" and "argumentative" are often misused within popular culture. "Argument" is often treated as a bad thing. But, like the term "rhetoric," argument can be bad or good. It depends on how it is being used. Argumentation merely provides a set of important communication tools. And we should embrace these tools. Like any set of tools, they can be used appropriately or inappropriately. Frequently, people misuse these argumentation tools. They use a sledge-hammer to drive a framing nail or a chainsaw to cut a toothpick. They yell when they should converse. They react impulsively when they should respond thoughtfully. However, as eloquent communicators, we will use argumentation appropriately. And we will not blame argument itself merely because other people do not know how to argue well.

Eloquent argumentation, and corresponding appeals to logos, requires a light touch, sophistication, and moderation. It embraces Aristotle's "golden mean." It seeks balance between excess and deficiency. Successful lawyers exemplify this moderate approach to argumentation. If lawyers are good, they communicate calmly, collectively, and strategically. Good lawyers can serve as role models for eloquent argumentation. It is a reason why courtroom deliberation dominates much of the discussions in Cicero's handbooks on rhetoric. In short, when applied with purpose and control, argumentation can be extremely useful to us in the workplace.

Although it may feel counterintuitive, eloquent argumentation proactively shields us. It provides armor to insulate us from foreseeable resistance. And it inspires courageous confidence in us. After all, in many ways, appeals to logos do not wait for assault or a glazed look on our listeners' faces. Argumentation does not wait for audiences to become confused. Rather, it anticipates and fortifies us against potential attack and misperception. By effectively communicating our stances, we can move ahead of explicit disagreement so that time (and energy) is not wasted on unnecessary combat. When we argue our stances responsibly, we will be able to civilly defuse disagreement. And we will cultivate cooperation, if resistance should arise.

Rather than relying on appeals to emotion, argumentative content provides direct means of shared rationality. As Aristotle shares in his *Rhetoric*, appeals to emotion can sometimes interfere with the focus of the discourse by leading audiences away from truth-seeking missions (1354a). Such misdirection can waste precious time. Tight argumentation, however, can logically cut through any misdirected noise. Tight argumentation immediately gets to the heart of the message. But first, we should gauge where audiences stand in relation to our argumentative goals.

Generally speaking, we encounter three types of audiences:

1. Resistant to our stance
2. Neutral or they do not know what to think
3. Lean toward our stance

As we discussed in Chapter 4 when discussing arrangement, several ingredients fuel an argument. When appealing to logos, we may highlight and more deeply develop these elements as they cooperate with our audience type. If we should choose to ignore certain parts, the choices should be deliberate. Any decision to leave out parts of our argument can still elevate our eloquence. After all, sometimes less is better. The practical ingredients of an argument are as follows:

1. Overarching stance/thesis of the message
2. Reasons that support why the stance/thesis is favorable or preferred
3. Evidence that supports each reason
4. Possible counterarguments to the overarching stance
5. Rebuttals to the respective counterarguments

Naturally, we do not have to use all of our rhetorical tools whenever we aim to persuade. If we choose to gloss over or ignore certain parts, these choices should be deliberate, and oriented toward efficiency. Because, again, sometimes less is better. For example, when speaking to agreeable audiences, we may use a few ingredients rather than all of them. Conversely, when addressing combative audiences, we may want to employ more from our rhetorical arsenal.

Appeals to logos provide reasons that support our stance. Rather than hiding our reasons, we can make them known to ensure they support our main point. As thoughtful communicators, we should determine how many reasons a situation calls for. Generally, more than one reason demonstrates the sophistication of our justification. However, we do not need to share all our reasons. To save time, we may cherry-pick the most compelling two or three reasons that support our position.

When addressing resistant audiences, we should concisely supply evidence. After each reason, evidence can demonstrate why each reason rings true. More than one piece of evidence helps prove that the reason is well supported. However, too many pieces of evidence can clutter the interaction. Typically, a maximum of two to three pieces of evidence for each reason avoids overwhelming the audience.

Additionally, when addressing resistant audiences, we may want to provide counterarguments, which is to say, how skeptics might "counter" our position. During this stage of our argument, we can voluntarily explain potential opposing positions and lines of opposing reasoning. After sharing these conflicting arguments, we rebut the counterarguments with reasoning and support. By acknowledging specific pressure points, we show how and why each counterargument is flawed. We counter the counterarguments.

Volunteering counterarguments can expand our communication. This tactic spends time to save time. Instead of waiting for possible counterarguments to be hurled at us by resistant audiences, we handle the counterarguments before our audiences can send our message spiraling away from its destination. We initially control the opposing position rather than allowing the audience to control it. This counterargument-and-reply tactic ultimately keeps us on-message like a rushing locomotive: direct and headstrong.

Let's examine an example of the mentioned argumentative ingredients, as applied to a skeptical readership. The following example comes from the body of a persuasive e-mail sent by a middle manager within a company. She seeks to persuade fellow colleagues about the value of holding a holiday office party during the Christmas season. Again, if the audience were more sympathetic to the holiday office party idea, the writer would supply less or no evidence and counterargumentation.

[...]

There are various reasons why we should hold a holiday office party for our team—but the strongest reason is because our team needs a Q4 morale boost. When we first considered the party back in October, I talked to several employees about the possibility, and their faces lit up. They told me that, after such a tough Q3, they would really appreciate a holiday party. They want to feel appreciated.

More specific to our holiday party, we can also announce Janice's upcoming January resignation. Apparently, experts say that it is best to announce resignations during some kind of joyous company get-together party (see attached Fast Company Magazine article for this information). And from my personal experience, I have found that holiday parties are great ways to transparently share news so that employees do not gossip.

Moreover, just as a comparison point, I talked to some of the management over at Hager Inc., our competitor, about their holiday parties. They love these parties. And they tell me that their employee morale remains strong.

Now I recognize that office parties can be expensive and can interfere with our tight budget. However, our administrative assistant is currently finding solutions to the financial constraints. Her initial report looks promising. I have supplied this report to this e-mail as well.

Overall, thanks for considering about a holiday party this year. It really feels like it would be a strong step in the right direction as we grow as a company.

A diagram of the e-mail:

Stance/Thesis: *We should hold a holiday office party for our employees.*
Reason One: *Because our team needs a Q4 morale boost.*
Support for R1: *I talked to several employees, and they told me that they would appreciate an office party. They want to feel appreciated.*
Support for R1: *Hager Inc. often holds holiday parties and their company morale remains strong.*

Reason Two: *A holiday party would be a great place to announce Janice's plans to resign in January.*

Support for R2: *Experts say that it is best to announce resignations at a joyous party.*

Support for R2: *And from my personal experience, I have always found that to be a great way to transparently share news so that employees do not gossip.*

Counterargument: *Office parties can be expensive and can interfere with our tight budget.*

Rebuttal: *However, our administrative assistant is currently finding solutions to the financial constraints. Her initial report looks promising.*

Repeat thesis and end with optimism: *Overall, a holiday party is a strong step in the right direction as we grow as a company.*

This e-mail strives for transparency. Consequently, both the writer and readers save time by avoiding prolonged back-and-forth quarreling. The writer anticipates potential disagreement and preemptively fortifies her position. Reasoning (asking and answering "why") provides the first line of defense, supporting the claim about the office party's reasonableness. Evidence (briefly proving each reason) serves as the second line of defense. If the audience doubts the validity of the reasons, some support bolsters them. If the audience remains unconvinced by the initial support, the writer can present additional supporting details. This type of communication can lead skeptics to acknowledge the plausibility of her perspective. Even if they do not change their beliefs, they may be persuaded by the reasonableness of her claims. Accordingly, they may be persuaded to continue the conversation.

Efficient Logic

Reasoning relies on the operations of logic. Since formal logic—as a discipline—offers an infinite array of maneuvers, this book will not delve deeply into all of the complexities. Logical machinery can be incredibly intricate, as evidenced by college logic textbooks, even the introductory textbooks. Fortunately, Aristotle's *Rhetoric* provides a shortcut to make logic more digestible for audiences. He offers some ways for both parties to save time.

Logical reasoning connects statements together to construct new knowledge and move things forward. To create something new, two statements need to collide in a manner that makes sense, producing a conclusion that also makes sense. Accordingly, logical proofs hinge on at least two premises, each relating to the other. This relational collision of claims formulates new insights.

As suggested earlier, numerous operational laws determine how claims relate to one another. Here, we will examine just one of these operations to illustrate how to condense our logic and save time. Let's begin with a simple logical law: *modus ponens*. In the following *modus ponens* structure, a major or general premise (line 1) relates to another minor or more specific premise (line 2) to form a conclusion (line 3):

1. If P, then Q.
2. P.
3. Therefore, Q.

This argument follows a *modus ponens* structure. To argue a particular conclusion, this basic setup can be highly effective. Let's apply *modus ponens* with a specific example: (1) If Saul has the flu, then he will not come into work. (2) Saul has the flu. (3) Therefore, Saul will not come into work. This simple example offers the logical structure outlined above.

Although this logic is basic, Aristotle offers a method to bridge this process without sacrificing logical operations. He suggests that rhetoricians champion the practical use of *enthymemes* (1356b5). *Enthymemes* streamline things. *Enthymemes* condense three terms (Premise 1, Premise 2, and Conclusion) into two terms (Premise 2 and Conclusion). Aristotle recognizes that in everyday communication, we are not so technical. Logic unfolds all the time in professional interactions, but often, we do not fully explain every logical maneuver. Instead, we omit a premise or two to streamline the message, assuming the audience already understands some of the underlying reasoning.

For example, instead of saying, "If Saul has the flu, then he will not come into work. Saul has the flu. Therefore, Saul will not come into work," we might simply say, "Saul has the flu, so he will not come into work." By condensing our arguments into two parts rather than three, we save time and space in our compositions, making our communication more direct and efficient.

Overall, we can intentionally avoid communicating certain logical steps. The logic still operates in our minds of listeners and readers; however, we do not present as explicitly within the message itself. The use of *enthymemes* depends on the audience's level of resistance. For a more resistant audience, we may want to avoid *enthymemes*. We may instead opt to patiently unpack every logical move and overtly justify the premises. Conversely, with a less resistant audience, we can save time by omitting claims that the audience already understands as true. This selective presentation balances clarity with efficiency. We tailor our approach to our audience's needs and expectations. While classical thinkers recognized these options back in the ancient world, today's workplace moves even faster. Therefore, the choice to appeal to logos, or not to appeal to logos, is even more crucial to our practical eloquence.

Keys to Practical Eloquence

Character matters. Foster confidence in character through practical insights, being charitable to listeners and readers, and being ethical-minded.

Persuade others via emotions. Think about the emotion itself, how that emotion can be modeled, and how that emotion is stirred in others. Use emotions ethically.

Appeal to logic and reality. When doing so, consider all of the logic and evidence, and then pick what would be most persuasive to share. Often, we don't need to share everything. If so, advantageously choose what logic and evidence to share.

Be *elegant* (appeal to a confident ethos), *eloquent* (wow our audience), and *relevant* (appeal to logic and reality).

CHAPTER 6

Savvy Storytelling

In the classical tradition, "poetics," that is, storytelling, plays nice with rhetoric and eloquence. That same collaboration still applies today. Strong storytelling adds vibrancy to our conversations, presentations, or documents. But what is story? And isn't story the same as "narrative"? In their book *Storynomics: Story-Driven Marketing in the Post-Advertising World*, Robert McKee (a celebrated screenplay writing coach and appreciator of the classical tradition) and marketing expert Thomas Gerace argue that "story" differs from "narrative." According to the authors, narrative offers a bland and vague sequence of events. In this sense, narrative aligns more closely to "plot." Story is much more vibrant, however. Story involves a dynamic unity of its parts: a combination of character, dialogue, setting, plot, tone, and theme. Story excites audiences and moves them to contemplate particular values.

Business and corporate communication professionals celebrate narrative from a different direction. To them, narrative offers not merely a component of story. Rather, narrative opens much larger avenues of storytelling. Narrative is open ended. According to his *Harvard Business Review* article "Every Company Needs a Narrative," John Hagel III explains that narrative involves "some kind of threat or opportunity looming in the future, and it's not at all clear how things are going to work out." He goes on to say, "the resolution of the narrative hinges on the choices and actions of those involved, which makes it a potentially powerful call to action." While a business can offer their own constantly evolving origin narratives, often narratives concern our customers or clients. Successful marketing invites target audiences into these larger narratives. Consequently, as Hegal recommends, building successful narratives requires a deep understanding of customers and clients: How are their needs evolving? What opportunities excite and inspire them? What challenges or obstacles would they confront in pursuing the opportunities?

What actions will they take to overcome obstacles to fulfill their desires? And are such actions something that our company helps them pursue?

It is no easy feat to craft inspiring customer/client-focused narratives. One of the best examples comes from Apple. In the 1990s, Steve Jobs articulated a narrative that became the slogan "Think different." The slogan communicates that other companies do not think in a bold "different" manner, but Apple does. Over time, Apple has shown this. "Thinking different" frames their narrative. To illustrate this boldness in their marketing, Apple consistently places themselves into history: emphasizing how they have improved technology over time. Apple is not the only company to use this narrative frame. Other companies have used it, as well, because it effectively brings customers into the narrative. After all, the company invites customers into history when buying their product. Buyers are not merely buying a product; they are accepting an invitation into an innovative history and future. In addition to Apple, General Electric offered this approach, too. In their 2002 "We Bring Good Things to Life" marketing campaign, GE emphasized how they have positively affected technological innovation. Through a montage of images and sound bites which emphasize advancement, their commercial tells the narrative of their company. They show past innovation and work, present innovation and work, and end with a hypothetical future image of a GE refrigerator on the moon.

In this way, stories act as part of narratives. Therefore, we do not need to pick either story or narrative when we professionally communicate, but instead, we can embrace both. While the narratives are broad and open-ended, stories act as evidence to support the greater narrative. We can tell brief anecdotes to evidence the narrative, or we can tell lengthier stories to bring our narratives more fully to life. For example, we can tell stories in our *exordiums* at the beginnings of presentations to hook audiences. We can tell stories during interviews to show a potential employer how we have personally handled a crisis or affected positive change. We can tell stories through our marketing to connect to customers and clients. The professional use of story is vast. But keep in mind that stories are embedded in larger unfolding narratives. Both stories and narratives were crucial to communication in the classical era. And they still are crucial today.

Driving Purposeful Stories

When told with stylistic flair, that is, when told *eloquently*, stories captivate and entertain. Stories transport audiences to specific moments in time, using well-paced drama and vivid details to recreate historical events. Effective storytelling moves beyond broad strokes of static information. They engage readers' or listeners' imaginations. By animating past historical events or future hypothetical events with words and images, we can guide audiences into collective visions.

That said, compelling stories bring events to life. Skilled storytellers can expand a single event into suspenseful before, during, and after sequences. Storytellers unfold events play-by-play, moment-by-moment. This expansive approach serves the story and, by extension, the evidential proof of a message.

According to Aristotle's *Poetics*, the six elements of storytelling are as follows: plot, character, spectacle, diction /dialogue, song, and thought. While he specifically uses these elements to discuss tragedy, we can stretch these elements to apply to storytelling in the professions.

Incentivize with Plot

Stories work well for several reasons. First, action grabs audiences' attention. The formal sequence of actions or events in a story is a plot. As Aristotle tells us in *Poetics*, plot propels a character into a story. Interesting plots act as pressure points or load-tests that challenge a story's characters, so audiences witness what characters do and how they react. Plots help audiences understand our characters' desires and their goal-seeking drives. Consequently, plot must keep characters on their toes. And by extension, plot must keep audiences on their toes. Events need to shift back and forth so that audiences do not get bored.

Aristotle provides simple structure of story to keep the action moving in interesting ways: the three-act plot. As business communication coaches, such as Carmine Gallo and Donald Miller, and screenplay writing coaches like Robert McKee and Blake Snyder point out, the three-act formula provides an intuitive way to structure story. While modern storytelling coaches appreciate the Three Act formula, the formula originally comes from Aristotle's *Poetics*. According to this tradition, Act One of a story involves the setup. It describes the everyday world of a protagonist and a catalyst event that spurs the protagonist's journey. Act Two is longer. It illustrates the journey of the protagonist that is antithetic to his or her previous Act One world. Act Three is the finale. It provides resolution to the overarching conflict. It synthesizes Act One and Two. In Act Three, the protagonist has changed and grown from the Act Two experiences in some way.

The three-act structure pervades marketing storytelling. Let's look at the late 1990s Chevy's "Like a Rock" advertising campaign for an example. In addition to playing the iconic song "Like a Rock" by Bob Seger in their television commercials, Chevy often told brief stories with their commercials: ones that featured their tough trucks in action. In one 1997 commercial, a man is frustrated that he cannot build a barn by himself (Act One). However, when he sees his friends drive their Chevy trucks up the hill toward him, he brightens up (move into Act Two). Smiling the entire time, his friends use their Chevy trucks to build a framework of a barn (Act Two). The commercial ends with the man and a woman (perhaps, a new love interest) both smiling and looking at the new frame of the barn as the sun sets (Act Three). The commercial begins with a problem, moves into a new world where his friends help the man build the barn, and ends with a new synthesis where they have created something new: the early framework of the barn and, presumably, a new relationship with a woman.

Overall, this type of problem–solution sequence frequents marketing and advertisement. A customer once didn't have a problem, but then their world is upended by a problem, and finally they solve it, specifically, through a product or service. It offers a Three Act formula. The structure is basic, but it frames many stories throughout history, including much of literature and film. It is familiar and commonplace. That is why it works so well. And the origins of these structures come from the ancient world.

Humanize with Characters

In a story, characters need to participate in the action. The characters can differ, depending on the story. The characters can include ourselves, clients, customers, founders of companies, or imaginary characters.

Audiences should identify with characters—so we need interesting, vivid characters. Like plot, the characters must be dynamic. They must grow, change, learn, go on transformative journeys, or face obstacles: preferably all of these things.

Aristotle also shares two ways to keep characters fresh. First, we should consider a pivotal moment in the story (often toward the end) where a main character's fortune is reversed. Something substantially changes outside of their control. The character may inherit a large sum of money; their business may be faced with bankruptcy; they may be bought out by a larger company. That reversal of fortune triggers the character's shift from ignorance to knowledge. Aristotle calls this second element the *recognition*. Through a recognition brought on by the reversal, the character learns and grows.

The classical tragedy *Oedipus Rex* offers an example of reversal and recognition. In *Oedipus Rex*, a tragic play by the ancient Greek dramatist, Sophocles, Oedipus experiences a profound reversal when a messenger tells him that that he unwittingly killed his father and married his mother, Jocasta. This realization is devastating for Oedipus. A once proud king, Oedipus experiences a recognition. He realizes that he should have more respect for the cosmic order of things, and more humility. While a tragedy, the play ends with wisdom and the promise of growth.

Workplace stories are not as dramatic as Sophocles' *Oedipus Rex*; however, they can still involve reversals and recognitions. For example, let's think about job interviews. Often in interviews, we share stories about times when we faced challenges. After we share these stories, we then share recognitions. In other words, we tell our interviewer what we have learned from the challenges or how we grew as professionals.

In addition to interviews, recognitions work within marketing. In marketing advertisement stories, characters often face problems because their fortunes have reversed. From these reversals, their recognitions conveniently pivot them toward the advertised product or service. For example, in a hypothetical commercial, the character of Jack is disappointed by a dish detergent that hasn't cleaned his dishes very well. But then he recognizes that our product, Cleano, can make his life easier and help reverse the reversal. Once Jack learns about our state-of-the-art Cleano dish detergent, he uses it, and his life becomes better. The advertisement's character Jack moves from ignorance (not knowing about our dish detergent) to knowledge (knowing about our dish detergent), and by extension, so does the viewer of the advertisement. As a result, like Jack, the viewer considers buying our dish detergent.

Ultimately, reversal and recognitions apply to characters. So, characters drive effective storytelling. Whether we tell stories about the origins of our business, stories about ideal customers visiting our website, or our personal stories to employers on job interviews, we should consider how we bring characters to life. After all, audiences connect to our characters since both audiences and characters share in being human. McKee provides some sage advice here. He tells us that we should seek three goals when communicating characters to audiences. First, we should *intrigue* audiences about our characters, so audiences have buy-in. Second, we should *convince* our audiences about our characters, so audiences believe in our characters' realness. Thirdly, we should *individualize* our characters so that the uniqueness of our characters pleases our audience. In other words, to use Cicero's *officia oratoris*, our stories' characters should move (intrigue), instruct (convince), and delight (individualize) our listeners or readers.

For example, we can tell story about Paul, a 32-year-old man who works in the Washington, D.C., region. In D.C., Paul is involved with politics, but he breaks away from the political life and distances himself from his toxic career. He relocates to Fargo, North Dakota, to join an up-and-coming communications consulting firm. The Fargo consulting firm gives him exactly the change he wants. While at the new firm, Paul teaches his team valuable perspectives that he learned from his time in Washington, D.C., which helps the firm flourish. At the same time, he learns about North Dakota culture from his North Dakota colleagues. Consequently, Paul embraces Fargo living, so he can healthily balance work with life. In this example, audiences may be intrigued by Paul's motivation for personal change; audiences may be convinced because Paul's struggle seems realistic and has the potential to teach transferable knowledge; and audiences may be delighted because Paul embarks on such a fascinating and successful adventure.

Dynamize with Spectacle

A spectacle is a visually striking scene or display. A spectacle engages the senses. Clearly, positive engagement with the senses is important to visual media like business websites or marketing efforts. And we will discuss this concept more deeply in Chapter 8 on aesthetics. However, how do we integrate spectacle into our storytelling? We can do this is a few ways. First, we can describe sensational scenes. For example, we can slow down the storytelling to describe a lavish London office building, a sizzling plate of fajitas, or a pristine suit of the CEO. Spectacle does not need to be as wild as that found in action films or high fantasy novels. Yet spectacle (if we ensure that it is reasonably spectacular) can be another tool to intrigue audiences about characters, the plot, or the story environment.

Just some words of caution about spectacle. First, Horace says we should probably not illustrate terrible scenes just for the spectacle (Lines 185–188). We should probably avoid describing disturbing or negative scenes in detail. They can be off-putting to audiences. Secondly, Aristotle warns us that our stories should not rely on spectacle too much (1453b6-7). Spectacle is more of a value-added element. Employing visual description can take our storytelling to the next level. While it is something we should consider, we should spend much more of our energy on plot and characters.

Crystallize with Dialogue

In addition to sensory details, dialogue vitally drives effective storytelling. Dialogue animates the characters, revealing their personalities through speech. It also places the audience directly within specific moments of the narrative. By accurately reciting or approximating what someone said, we create a second-by-second, word-for-word reenactment of scenes. Dialogue brings historical reality to life in the minds of the audience, acting as a crucial temporal element that connects the story to our readers or listeners.

Through dialogue we can hear *from* our characters, not merely learn *about* characters. Dialogue helps crystallize the human energy of our stories, so audiences connect to our characters. However, taking McKee's advice, we should ensure that our dialogue individualizes our characters, and intrigues and convinces audiences about our characters. If not, the dialogue can feel forced, unnatural, or cliché. It will not help our story. And it may poorly reflect on our storytelling abilities or the abilities of our business. So, if we use dialogue, ensure that we do it well.

Beautify with Song

As mentioned in the Introduction chapter, people appreciate musicality and song. Aristotle notes that song is important in story as well. That said, times have changed since ancient Greece. We no longer have groups of singing choruses within our stories like ancient Greek theater. Yet we still have musical theater and film scores. So, music has be reappointed within story. It has not altogether disappeared. Song and music still have a place.

How does this help us in workplace with business storytelling? We can embrace the music of language: diction, rhyme, sentence rhythm, and balance. If we do it effectively, our sentences can sing. As a result, parts of our story can stick in people's minds. A catchy line in a story is like that song we hear in the airport or dentist's office. You know, the ones that we can't get out of our heads the entire day? Through musical lines, we can craft our own earworms.

As an expression of order, music is easily remembered. When compounded with the memorable Three Act order of a story, musical language can help people remember key themes or messages from our stories. Specifically, catchy phrasings help especially in marketing or training stories. Clever wording pleases and delights audiences while also engaging the memory. For example, we may tell a story about a company team who landed an important client and made the client happy, and we end that story with "Remember, everyone: we chase the dream as a team." Or we may conclude more subtly through alliteration: "Remember, folks: clients welcome collaboration." In short, we know that catchy taglines work well in marketing. We can offer the same approach when wrapping up a story. We can add moments of melody. We can add moments of song.

Optimize with Thought

According to Aristotle, good stories should communicate thought or theme. In other words, stories do more than merely entertain. They drive home a point. They illustrate reality, values, or the human condition in particular ways. Granted, stories that we tell in business contexts may not be as profound as those of Homer, Sophocles, or Virgil, but still we should keep Aristotle's "thought" in the back of our minds. Stories should do something purposeful in our communication. They should appeal to deeper principles or ideas. Doing so contributes to the eloquence of the story. As previously mentioned, Apple and GE have done this in their marketing: they emphasize the values of innovation and the technological progress that drive history. On a more personal level, if we tell a story about how we turned around our small business during the hardships of COVID-19, we promote values of perseverance and grit.

While classical drama often explicitly tells audiences the message or "thought" at the end of a tragedy (such as in Sophocles' *Antigone*) or comedy (such as, in Aristophanes' *The Clouds*), we do not have to be so blatant. The story itself can communicate "thought" by showing and not telling. But we should read our audience. Are listeners picking up what we are putting down? If not, then we may want to tell them. And writing may differ from speaking here. We may be more willing to explicitly tell them our "thought" behind a story when we write. After all, as Plato recognizes in the *Phaedrus* (274c–277a), we may not be able to closely know the audience who reads our writing. Or we may know our reader, but we do not know their state of mind when they read it. And we want to ensure that they "get" our meaning. So, we may consider explicitly telling them what written stories mean after we share them, and why that matters.

Story as Evidence

Now that we have explored the elements of story, how does story more specifically get things done? Stories, both real and hypothetical, are powerful tools for sharing examples. In other words, stories help us effectively share evidence. For instance, if we tell a colleague that a rival company is strong, we can tell a story about the competitor's business which illustrates its strength. If we mention an ideal type of customer for our business, we can tell a hypothetical story about this ideal customer. Ultimately, whether lengthy yarns or short anecdotes, stories engage the audience's imagination. As such, they make evidence more memorable and enjoyable. By rhetorically and poetically crafting these stories, we transform dry facts into active demonstrations. By blending the art of storytelling with strategic communication, we enhance the impact of our messages, so they can be both memorable and meaningful.

Creative nonfiction, also known as literary journalism, brightly illustrates real events through artistic narratives. This form of storytelling does not distort the truth; rather, it presents reality in a gripping and dramatic way. Over the decades, esteemed authors like Truman Capote, Joan Didion, Tom Wolfe, and David Sedaris have mastered this craft. They have published powerful synergies to inform, instruct, and delight. As these authors reveal, creative nonfiction combines factual accuracy with literary artistry. They transform real events into compelling narratives. And we can do the same thing. By utilizing sensory details and dialogue, we can create similarly immersive experiences that deeply resonate with audiences.

Hypotheticals: Probable Stories

We can also employ future-directed stories to engage our audiences. These stories are hypotheticals. Naturally, unproven or fabricated stories may problematize our interactions or writing. However, these types of stories can still serve professional communication if used appropriately. Hypothetical projections allow us to make up stories if they are plausible. Specifically, hypothetical stories trace potential events that have not occurred but *could reasonably happen*. Hypotheticals are possible scenarios that encourage audiences to consider possible future outcomes, providing intriguing perspectives on the subject matter.

For instance, to a business partner, we may argue that we should hire professional painters to paint our office lobby. In promoting this course of action, we might tell a cautionary tale about the risks of *not* hiring painters. We may tell a hypothetical story about the risks when attempting to paint the lobby *ourselves*. In the story, we may mess up the paint job so bad that the lobby must be repainted *again*. In this scenario, time and money are thereby wasted. And we can narrate this negative possibility in vivid detail. So, even if we don't have hard evidence to support our claims, we can craft a hypothetical story about a botched paint job that feels real. By illustrating this scenario with sensory details and dialogue, we demonstrate the potential risks involved. To that end, we can persuade our business partner to hire professional painters rather than painting the room ourselves.

Hypotheticals do not only correspond to bad possibilities. We can tell hypotheticals about pleasant futures as well. Hypothetical stories may allow our employees, clients, or customers see better futures for themselves and others. Therefore, we can tell vivid stories to persuade others about a brighter future of our company, customers' improved lives when they use our product, or a better world with our company in it. In this way, the stories drive optimistic open-ended narratives.

Of course, we should be careful when telling hypothetical tales. First, we must not confuse our possible stories with true events, and we need to ensure that our audience understands the distinction. After all, these mix-ups can lead to misinformation. Therefore, it is our responsibility to clearly signal that a story is hypothetical. Using transitional tags like, "Imagine if ..." or "It could be possible that ..." communicates that the evidence is not real. At the same time, it still offers the story as a plausible future scenario.

Additionally, we should be careful of slippery slope arguments. Slippery slope arguments project a chain of increasingly extreme hypothetical events that stem from relatively mild setups. For example, we may argue that hiring professional painters to paint our lobby is valuable. Why? It's safer than painting ourselves because we may fall from a ladder and become paralyzed. This story veers into unlikely and extreme territory. Slippery slope arguments can rely on fear rather than logic. They can deliberately misrepresent improbable severe situations as probable ones. This technique may undermine the argument and our credibility as a communicator.

That said, sometimes events may indeed warrant slippery slopes. For example, a spelling error in a web advertisement may cause our customers to doubt our competence which can lead to many customers switching to a competitor whereby we suffer catastrophic financial losses. Overall, it depends on the circumstances and the parties involved. Depending on the situation and the nature of the spelling error, a spelling error could indeed lead to such catastrophe. In short, a chain of events may be a reasonable slippery slope. As storytellers, we should gauge the reasonability of hypothetical sequences before sharing them.

To responsibly use hypotheticals, we should avoid evoking extreme emotions and instead share honest, reasonable outcomes. This approach helps audiences think productively about the future, encouraging them to consider plausible scenarios without fearmongering. By judiciously using hypothetical situations, we enhance our arguments and engage our audience in thoughtful, forward-facing ways.

Fictional Stories: Beyond Hypotheticals

If told well, fictional stories can be pleasurable experiences. We may indulge in Danielle Steel's romance novels at the beach, read Stephen King's short stories during long plane rides, or watch streaming Netflix shows on rainy Friday nights. We choose to engage with these made-up stories because, although they can be fantastic, they resonate with our reality in meaningful ways. Fiction, including science fiction and fantasy, rearranges our reality and returns it to us through compelling stories. While the stories are made up, they still communicate general truths that woo and teach audiences. While it is difficult to use spectacle in real-life stories, fictional stories often highlight spectacle much more because they are not real. Through fiction, we can also exaggerate to please the senses, hook readers or viewers, and eventually move or instruct them.

Fictional stories craft imaginative worlds. These worlds' events, operations, and characters are plausible within their contexts. Often, successful fictional stories are relatable because they touch on dimensions of our own realities. They propel us to think, "If I were in the same situation as this fictional character, what would I do?" In this way, the stories are analogical. By inspiring such questions, fictional stories function as imaginative hypothetical situations that operate within their own artificial frameworks. As a result, fictional stories serve as creative thought experiments that aid instruction and persuasion.

This technique echoes the methods of ancient storytellers like Homer and Virgil. Homer's *Odyssey* and Virgil's *Aeneid* are not merely epic tales of adventure. They offer profound reflections on nature, virtue, and the human condition. Aristophanes' comedies are not merely stories to make us laugh. Through irony, they offer profound insights into how not to behave. Sophocles' and Euripides' tragedies are not merely stories to sadden us. They offer profound reflections on wisdom and ethics. In short, these stories, while fictional, connect deeply with audiences' understandings of reality. They prompt audiences to consider their own values and virtues. Just as Odysseus' trials and Aeneas' journeys resonate with timeless human experiences, fiction invites audiences to explore and reflect upon their own lives. Aristotle's "thought" links the fiction to reality. As such, a story's "thought" can help a fictional story communicate general truths or lessons in the business world.

In addition to appealing to logos, fiction appeals to pathos. Marketing guru Seth Godin understands fictional storytelling as a profound tool to boost sales. According to Godin's *All Marketers Are Liars*, fictional narratives allow marketers to craft compelling "what if" scenarios to captivate the audience's imagination. These stories, while not true in a literal sense, convey deeper human desires. They help audiences not just envision potential futures, but, more importantly, fictional stories help audiences *feel* those potential futures. They see themselves within those scenarios and feel the experiences. This engagement makes the message more relatable and impactful. Godin emphasizes that fictional stories help bypass consumer skepticism. Instead, they engage emotional cores of target customers and foster trust and loyalty. Through the emotive dimensions of fiction, marketers inspire action and drive change. They transform abstract ideas into lived experiences within minds of audiences.

Presencing

Storytelling is a powerful way to "presence" evidence within our arguments. In their 1958 handbook on argumentation, *The New Rhetoric*, Chaim Perelman and Lucie Olbrechts-Tyteca explore how presence heightens rhetorical connectivity. They suggest that when we presence the reality of a topic within a conversation, we imbue that topic with importance. Therefore, it becomes our task to presence any claim that cannot be materially evidenced through, what they call, "verbal magic alone." In other words, eloquent communicators "show" and do not merely "tell." By combining showing and telling, our verbal magic can materialize particular claims within compositions. Stories can perform that verbal magic.

For example, consider a workplace conversation at the water cooler. Here, Alexa tells her colleague Hunter that she is having a wonderful day. Hunter may believe her or not. Her claim has yet to be presenced. However, as soon as Alexa describes how her wonderful day unfolded, how she received a raise, landed three new clients, and won $45 from a scratch-off lottery ticket, Hunter is more inclined to believe her. Through this presenced evidence, Hunter adheres more closely to the message as Alexa escorts him into the presence of her claims. Furthermore, if Alexa narrates the three wonderful events with vivid, play-by-play storytelling, Hunter's belief deepens. He believes her even more. Why? Because storytelling acts as a presencing mode. When Alexa tells stories to vividly depict her evidence in action, Hunter becomes transported into reliving those past events alongside her. She becomes present within his imagination. The way Alexa stylizes her evidence and stories play a rhetorical role in transporting Hunter to a present moment within the message. This "verbal magic" acts as presencing rhetoric and eloquence.

Whether we offer material evidence in our storytelling to presence a claim or we invite our audience to be present alongside us in the interaction (or optimally, both), heightening the present moment in time is central to eloquent communication. Ultimately, a goal of eloquence is to commune with our audience within a present moment. The more presence that we weave into our interactions, the more our audience is "with us." Presence optimizes the clarity of the message and the warmth of human-to-human interaction. By weaving presence into our eloquence, we not only communicate more effectively, but also build stronger, more empathetic connections with our audiences. Storytelling does much of that heavy lifting.

As mentioned in a previous chapter, humans bond and connect over shared crises. Stories work well because they often communicate artificial, hypothetical, or past crises. Remember, crises are found in the Act Two of the classical plot structure, and those crises are resolved in Act Three of the story. The audience bonds with the storyteller because they experience the story's Act Two crisis together within the safe arena of their imagination. And audiences are relived when the crisis is resolved in Act

Three. This phenomenon may explain why the classical plot design is so persuasive. After all, the classical structure presences characters' crises so audiences can connect to them.

A story's crisis underscores the powerful connective force of shared adversity. As Aristotle noted in his *Rhetoric*, emotions such as fear and hope can profoundly impact the bonds formed between individuals. In moments of emergency, these shared emotions create unique, almost primal connections. These moments can facilitate trust and camaraderie among strangers. Much like how Greek tragedies or Roman epics unite audiences through shared emotional experiences, modern crisis stories, lived or told, unite us in our common humanity. It can unite managers to their teams, clients to businesses, and customers to companies. But we must always remember to drive toward an Act Three: a resolution, or at the very least, a move toward resolution. This way, we as storytellers and our audiences seek to win together.

Keys to Practical Eloquence

Stories work within larger narratives. Consider how the stories operate in these grander and more open-ended narratives. Perhaps stories work in our own personal narratives or in companies' narratives.

Stories offer more than entertainment. Stories move, teach, and delight. Therefore, they evolve our eloquence toward greater impact.

Consider multiple elements within story: plot, character, dialogue, spectacle, song, and thought. Balance them and use them thoughtfully within all types of stories, large or small.

Use stories to point to the past or imagine possible futures. Use stories to presence the evidence of claims in powerfully vivid and memorable ways.

CHAPTER 7

The Dance of Dialectics

What is the dialectic? Ultimately, dialectic empowers purposeful, truth-seeking conversation. According to Aristotle and Plato, the dialectic drives logical reasoning. It offers us a procedure to convey our reasoning to others, and then, receive others' reasoning in return. It is a method of reasoning together toward higher level insights. Through the dialectic, people trade plausible points of view back and forth and refine those opinions closer to truth.

The energy of the dialectic is paramount. The *New World Encyclopedia* defines dialectical movement as volleying between parties which resembles slalom in skiing. The movement veers right, then left, then right again, and so on, but the overall direction is straight ahead.

Ultimately, *the dialectic ensures that our communication stays in the realm of influence, not manipulation.* We do not want to steamroll others toward narrow one-sided opinions or even misinformed falsehoods. Classical dialectic helps insulate our communication against these possible missteps. It helps us engage socially with others. And it helps us kindle warm conversations rather than preach or lecture to others. To that end, the dialectic balances purposeful cooperation with healthy competition.

Thinking dialectically, and outwardly, communicating dialectically, opens our options as speakers and writers. When expressing contrary positions, people often think that we have two options: (1) win-win compromise where both parties sacrifice their perspective to meet in the middle, or (2) a zero-sum game where one party wins. But can there be a third option? What if two-parties both win without compromise? After all, what if two parties can mutually agree that something is true, and they do not need to settle on a partial compromise? Can't they establish a full win-win and land on something that is true for both parties? In doing so they work dialectically. How so? They either arrive at something true, or something that closely approximates truth itself. In a way, the approach resembles how two scientists may volley points of view back and forth to figure out what is true. Their shared pursuit is not about the scientists' egos but about the reality outside of them. We seem to think that this truth-seeking approach only applies to the hard sciences. However, the modern hard sciences emerged out of classical philosophy. And classical philosophy emerged from the Sophists, Socrates, and Plato who were all dialecticians.

The dialectic offers a way to seek truth. It requires maneuverability, which is a type of dance. So rather than a one-sided speech or unidirectional document, the dialectic insists on social interaction. The classical dialectic in the Socratic tradition requires not just competition between two perspectives but additionally it requires cooperation and goodwill between parties. It balances both perspectives so that each dancer can contribute and shine. Yet it also allows the dancing duo to shine as a unit, too. Consequently, the spirit of the dialectic does not have a winner. And it also refuses to take "agree to disagree" as an answer.

Let's first consider the strategic relation between cooperation and competition and then get into some classical tactics.

Cooperative Competition

Toward the end of Homer's epic *Iliad*, Greek soldiers partake in "funeral games" after Patroclus dies at the hands of Hector and the Trojans. To celebrate the life of their friend and warrior, the Greeks hold a series of competitions to rank their skills, such as footraces, chariot-races, and archery contests. Each competition places first, second, and third place winners. The games are clearly competitive. But they offer a united celebration to not only remember the excellence of their fallen comrade Patroclus, but also to celebrate excellence overall as a team. The games are both fun and serious. They deliver entertainment with underlying gravity.

The dialectic demands similar type of harmony between competition and cooperation, play and work. Brandenburger and Nalebuff's influential 1997 game theory book *Co-opetition* can provide insight into the harmonization process. The authors suggest that business relationships can be "complementary," not always at odds. Communication offers similar complementarity. What is complementarity exactly? Brandenburger and Nalebuff illustrate complementarity in various business contexts. The authors share one example that involves technology: computer software and computer hardware. Each is contingent on the other and therefore, each complements the other. Heightened computer hardware requires heightened computer software; heightened computer software requires heightened computer hardware. In the computer business, each market can cooperate with the other. They are not in outright competition. Despite their differences, competitors carry each other toward new business and insights so that each party benefits.

Like successful open-minded business practices, every interaction does not need to be a war. Brandenburger and Nalebuff describe this warring attitude as a Jekyll and Hyde relationship. They posit that unfortunately many businesspeople see others as evil "Mr. Hydes" rather than complementary "Dr. Jekylls." Instead of seeing all competitors as bloodthirsty monsters, players in the game can smartly complement one another. By observing complementary opportunities in business relations, businesses can thrive via cooperative win-win dynamics rather than all-or-nothing trade-off dynamics.

Successful communication unfolds by acting on similar win-win situations. An eloquent communicator wins by being understood by an audience; the audience wins by clearly understanding an eloquent message. The communicator wins by relationally delivering their message to a receptive audience; the audience wins by relationally receiving a thoughtful communicator. Then, in the spirit of the dialectic, the parties reverse their roles. The speaker becomes the listener, and the listener becomes the speaker. Within optimal processes of dialectical discourse, each side cooperatively helps advance the progress of new insights. Consequently, each party should essentially win because each side unearths knowledge, or at the very least, trades information in pursuit answers and practical solves.

Dialectical communication seeks this kind of relational win-win. Dialectical communication is not only about getting what we want, such as the satisfaction from completely persuading an audience or the joy felt from expressing ourselves. Rather, dialectical communication balances an audience's win with our win. This balance is one of the most overlooked elements that I encounter when I read student work or when I consult on professional manuscripts. Writers can sometimes forget the audience's *reading* experience and privilege their own *writing* experience. Writers may emphasize what they have to say and lose track of their audience's experience. These writers find it difficult to think outside of themselves to enact their communicative vision. We should avoid falling into that trap. The relationship between the writer and reader should optimally aim for a dialectical relationship.

Maneuvering with Resistant Audiences

Once we become receptive to working with others in our communicative interactions, we still may hit another obstacle: others may not be receptive to working with us. They may be difficult to work with. In the practical world, we do not always face neutral or welcoming audiences. Sometimes we face resistant audiences. These audiences can range from quiet skeptics to boisterous contrarians. These people will not agree with our claims, information, attitudes, or values. Occasional resistance is natural; after all, we all have different ideas and perspectives. It is naive to think that communication never involves conflict.

So, what is a solution? These interactions may involve warring attitudes. However, we should try to resist thinking about who is going to "lose." And try to think of both parties winning. Instead of seeing conflicted communication as strategic war, perhaps think of it as a strategic training ground. Rather than thinking of it as bloody life-or-death battle outside of castle walls, we can think about it as hand-to-hand combat training with wooden swords inside the safety of castle walls. We can think about it as play.

If the wooden swordplay analogy does not work for us, perhaps we can consider discussions with resistant audiences as friendly chess games with a friend or relative where we seek to better learn the game and become better players. Again, this self-edification approach helps see our interactions as play. What is the advantage of play? Play relieves stress. The "play perspective" relinquishes the pressure of needing to win the day, which can ward off temptations to manipulate our audiences. If we think of conflicted communication as a game, we can save ourselves from being too pushy. Furthermore, the training ground approach also helps moderate emotional responses. We calmly replace fiery tendencies with appropriate rationality.

If we see communication as a training ground, we can learn from others and improve our communicative strategies for future interactions. It offers an arena to learn and develop at the art of communication. Specifically, if communication situations do not unfold as desired, think about what we can learn from these interactions to help us in the future. All is not lost. Through the failed communication interactions, we can learn something to potentially save us in future communication interactions, if, of course, we adopt growth mindsets and recognize learnable takeaways.

Resistant audiences may disagree with our ideas but as was established in the early chapters, communication is an art. Therefore, despite disagreement, we can still make an audience feel good with how we strategically frame and deliver our ideas. As will be discussed in Chapter 8 on aesthetics, a message's constructed internal unity helps build plausibility, reasonability, and likeability. Whereas war is set up to have a winner and a loser, communication (as shared common duty) promotes middle ground. This mindset can help disarm temptations to blitzkrieg others with our perspectives. We do not have to always convert others wholesale (a difficult ask). Rather, our communication approach can usher others toward the reasonable positions as situated in reality (a manageable ask). This method of realistic communication helps facilitate controlled eloquent persuasiveness and fosters approachability and likeability.

Invite the Yes and No

Both Daniel H. Pink and Robert Cialdini both agree that contrast helps people better understand an idea. We understand something better when it is held against something different than when it stands alone or floats in a vacuum. Cialdini calls this the "contrast principle." He explains that a "jolt of the unfamiliar" shakes up how we see things. We see it from another angle. It wakes us from our complacent slumber. When we invite contrast, we invite that wake-up call.

This frame by contrast is not a modern concept. It can be traced back to Plato and Aristotle. In his discussion of truth, Aristotle tells us that we better understand that something is true by understanding what something is and by understanding what something is not (1011b25-30). To better understand, we should grasp what it is and that it is—and what it is not and that it is not (1011b25-30). We should seek the yes and no. In the early Middle Ages, this contrast was embraced, too. In the 1110s, Peter Abelard wrote *Sic et Non*, an early scholastic text whose title translates from Medieval Latin as "Yes and No." In the work, Abelard contrasts contradictory quotations from the Church on many philosophical and spiritual topics. Clearly controversial for the time, he highlights the contradiction but then resolves them. Abelard's approach is dialectical. We can embrace a similar approach: Embrace the yes and the no and seek to resolve them—yet do so without completely eliminating one or the other.

In Mark H. McCormack's 1984 book on deal-making, negotiations, and sales *What They Don't Teach You at Harvard Business School*, he concisely notes a sales strategy that may seem counterintuitive: "People have a need to say no. So let them. [...] Collect some negative currency before you get to whatever it is that you really want to sell." He explains, "A few well-placed 'no's' create the right environment for a 'yes.'" Therefore, we can allow the opposing position to provide their perspective and their reasoning. This way, others can be heard, and we do not steamroll them. We should authentically weigh their reasoning, too. If our position still stands, we can reply back to their argument. The approach resembles what we discussed in Chapter 4 on arrangement. We can admit and embrace working with counterarguments.

Even if we disagree with other parties, we can also establish a yes before a no. For example, the Stoic philosopher Seneca consistently praised Epicurus, a philosopher who supported hedonism. Stoicism (resisting pleasures) literally opposes hedonism (embracing pleasures). Seneca opposed all of Epicurus' ideas, but in Seneca's letters, he constantly praises Epicurus' character. According to Seneca, Epicurus had a good character; it was Epicurus' *ideas* that he didn't agree with. Seneca provided a yes and a no without compromising his own ideas. As such, Seneca appears balanced and reasonable, and does not compromise his convictions.

While Aristotle tells us that the yes and no help us better understand, and while Seneca's comments illustrate a yes and no in action, Plato shows the yes and no in action even more. Throughout his dialogues, Plato features characters who often assume contrary sides of arguments. Rather than merely debate the issue, the characters work together through different perspectives to arrive at what is true. In some arguments, characters resist one another a bit more; other dialogues, characters discourse more passively and allow the confident truth-seeker of Socrates to lead the discussion.

Socratic Method

The Socratic method is a method of questioning and reasoning used by the character of Socrates in Plato's classical dialogues. Since the dialogues are fictional interactions, we do not know how close the character of Socrates resembles the real Socrates. The historical Socrates can may be considered one of the more sincere members of the Sophists. According to Plato's dialogues, Socrates was more committed to truth-seeking than other Sophists from his time. Today, his approach to dialectical thinking is valuable to philosophers and lawyers, but it can also be quite valuable to us as business professionals. The Socratic method drives us to better understand a matter at hand and think more rationally.

The Socratic method enacts the dialectic. According to Socrates in *Phaedrus*, dialecticians surgically divide content by carving up ideas "form by form according to its natural joints and trying not to hack through any part as a bad butcher might" (265e). So, dialecticians look closely at the ideas without distorting them. And they also merge content by bringing into "a single form things which have been previously scattered in all directions" (265d), so they combine different ideas together where they naturally cooperate. In short, Socrates praises this overall dialectical process for how it divides and generalizes, how it unites and pluralizes, which ultimately helps him speak and think well (266b).

The dialectic as enacted through the Socratic method can help us speak, write, and think well, too. For example, imagine that we are hiring to fill a position. First, we think about the crucial parts of the task. What are the dimensions of the job? What are the *most important* dimensions of the job? Who are the candidates? What are their attributes? How does each candidate fulfill the dimensions of the job? Ultimately, we direct our attention toward the parts of the job call and the characteristics of the candidates; then we unite candidates to the job call. In the spirit of the dialectic, we break apart our concepts and then unite them. While Plato explores philosophical concepts by thinking about how concepts differ and what concepts share, we can be more practical with the dialectic. The break-apart-and-unite approach still works. After all, both Plato's processes and our processes still aim for logical answers.

We can perform this dialectical process mentally by ourselves or socially with others. For example, Augustine wrote dialectical dialogues, such as the *Soliloquies*, where he would exchange questions and reasoning with a character named "Reason." This way, instead of writing straightforward treatises on a subject, he would display his internal dialogue about a subject and illustrate the back-and-forth reasoning on the page. Readers can then follow Augustine's logical moves through a dynamic dialogue. Earlier in the classical era, Plato's dialogues depicted Socrates speaking with different characters and pursuing answers to philosophical questions. Plato's dialogues read more like literature where characters speak dialectically to one another. Overall, the choice is up to us. We can work dialectically in our own heads as individuals. Or we dialectically interact more socially with others. Or perhaps both.

As pointed out, the dialectic is optimally fueled by the Socratic method. And the use of questions drives the Socratic method. Therefore, when we try to discover a large answer or arrive at a macro-level solution, we should ask ourselves or others small questions and patiently work up from there. The response from each question should specifically fuel another question that fuels another question, and so on. In this way, it creates a chain of reasoning through the conversation between two people with different perspectives.

To return to a previous example, when hiring for a web designer position, the dialectical approach requires that we shouldn't jump to the question, Who will be the best fit? Rather, we should rather think more patiently and fundamentally. Dialectically, we should first define our terms and ask, What does it mean to be an employee? What is the role of a company? Then, what does it take to be an employee of *our* company?

Then, what does it mean to be a good web designer? And develop the reasoning from this foundation. So, the proceeding conversation depends on how the questions are answered. In short, with the Socratic method, foundational terms and ideas are established before leafing through the pool of candidates, and especially before committing to one ideal candidate. Being more patient and dialectical with our reasoning, we can carefully trace the logic, so the final choice of candidate fully matches the criteria, and we are more soundly justified in our decision.

The Socratic method also pivots upon consistency. Its questions probe for inconsistency. If one party's answers are inconsistent with previous answers, we should recognize this, ask why, and reshape the conversation in pursuit of consistency. For example, let's say that the hiring team establishes that web design work experience is the primary criterion of a new hire. But, after interviewing candidates, a colleague states that candidate A should be hired because she has a calm demeanor. Inconsistency has emerged. The main criterion is not "calm demeanor" but "web design experience." In this way, our colleague has ignored the logic. And it needs to be resolved. Either the criterion needs to be reworked, candidate A needs to be reconsidered, or our colleague's logic is skewed.

In short, Socratic consistency keeps us on task. In this way, Socratic consistency flies in the face of more modern relativistic perspectives where we "agree to disagree." It allows consensus to emerge from dissensus. Using reason and dialogue, either socially or individually, the Socratic method seeks answers as they correspond to reality. By dialectically seeking consistency, we will eventually discover the best candidate in a pool of candidates. And strong reasoning would support our choice.

Keep the Conversation Going

We have all ended professional conversations with, "Let's keep the conversation going!" It is a productive way to say goodbye in the workplace. It implies that a line of communication will remain open. It signals that we are happy to speak again.

Similarly, the classical dialectical process offers a way to keep the conversation going. After all, if every dialectical response can be further questioned, the process should never end. In the same spirit of keeping the conversation alive, the dialectic aligns with two principles:

1. As human beings, we are limited in our reasoning. Therefore, we cannot fully know everything the cosmos offers. But we should not be discouraged by these limitations. Instead, these limitations should keep us hungry to chase knowledge.
2. We should continue to pursue excellence. Even if we land on a solution, a better solution probably exists. So, we should keep the line of communication open to refine the solution. If we reach an impasse with someone, we should discourse dialectically until we establish some smaller points that we agree on. Then we can use those smaller points as jumping-off points and proceed from there.

In short, we should not seek to suffocate conversation by pretending to have answers. Rather, we should open up our conversations in productive ways. And this applies to sales as well. Daniel H. Pink explains that sales pitches have changed over the decades. In the past, salespeople had to be skilled at accessing information and providing answers. But now, because of the Internet and smartphones, information is at everyone's fingertips. Consequently, salespeople must be skilled at "curating" information to assist with clarity and relevance. And Pink tells us effective curation depends on asking customers or clients effective questions to "uncover possibilities." Ultimately, good modern salespeople dialectically converse with customers or clients, so they pursue the best solutions together. In the spirit of cooperative competition, the Socratic method can assist this process. Therefore, according to Pink's insight about sales, the classical dialectic serves sales today more than in the immediate past. The relevance of the dialectic shows how the practical wisdom of ancient philosophers and rhetoricians still rings true and fosters success in the modern era. So, if we want to be eloquent salespeople, we should read Plato, imitate Socrates, and we will be moving in the right direction.

Keys to Practical Eloquence

Like the *Iliad*'s funeral games, the dialectic offers a playful sort of gravitas. Take conversation seriously but playfully ask questions about the subject matter to better understand.

Dialectic focuses on a refined process of arriving at solutions. The process shouldn't be rushed. Use the Socratic method to break down and synthesize concepts through the question-and-answer discourse. Seek to pursue consistency, as well. Trust the patient process that may take some time. Yet the time spent is rewarding. It leads to more transparent understandings and sounder solutions.

Practicing dialectical conversation (and listening or reading dialectical dialogue) results in stronger critical thinking skills. The Socratic method can be (and should be) seen as a superpower in the professions. It strengthens more lucid and clear eloquence.

CHAPTER 8

Beautify Your Message

Today's digital multimedia world sings and dances with flashiness. We are immersed in environments with innovative messaging: GIFs, animations, streaming videos, virtual reality, augmented reality, and pithy memes. Visual social media sites like TikTok and Instagram have gained popularity, especially with younger people, and have surpassed writing-based platforms like Facebook and Twitter. Much to Plato's disappointment, dazzling online appearances are increasingly sought after as "ends in themselves." And we are all guilty of gravitating toward the glamour. We are all guilty of being hypnotized by striking pictures, videos, and website designs like awe-filled infants entranced by multi-colored crib toys.

As a university professor, I've noticed the strong power of alluring visuals with my students. Eye-catching appearances, such as pictures, videos, flashy colors, and bright lights, mesmerize students in the college classroom. When a professor verbally delivers material with eloquence, energy, and passion, half or three-quarters of the students may pay attention, depending on the student population and culture. Yet, as soon as the professor queues up a video or picture, one hundred percent of students' heads pop up. They stare the image on the screen. Their eyes grow wide. They lean forward with anticipation.

Visual presentation acts as "window dressing" to attract attention while also enhancing the experience and supporting understanding. If we make that window dressing beautiful, we can do all of this even better. This use of aesthetics is what we will consider in this chapter.

Beauty Is Not "In the Eye of the Beholder"

As we've previously discussed, rhetorical business communication seeks to grab people's attention and maintain it. Eloquence does the same but offers something else: sophistication and beauty.

Again, aesthetics is the study of beauty. The fact that aesthetics offers us a studied discipline implies that there is indeed something rich to study. In other words, if beauty were arbitrary, which is to say, solely "in the eye of the beholder," such study wouldn't really be necessary. In support of a fuller understanding of beauty, we can observe the following point: every one of us finds Mozart, Bach, or Vivaldi's classical music to be beautiful. We may not listen to classical music regularly. But certainly, we all appreciate the music. We can all recognize it is beautiful in some way. There is something universal about this beauty. There is something that extends across time and cultures.

The same observation applies to natural scenes of beauty. For example, we can all surely appreciate breathtaking Florida sunsets which radiate vibrant pinks, soft purples, and bright yellows. While some of us may not like Florida as a region or we may not regularly watch sunsets, we can all appreciate the splendor of the sunset. Again, something about the beauty is universal. The sunset offers beauty that can be perceived across time and cultures.

Conversely, we can agree on what is not beautiful. We can generally agree that a refrigerator's hum, a car's exhaust, a person coughing, or a blank bathroom wall is not beautiful. And the lack of beauty can extend across time and cultures, too.

The classical tradition believes that while some subjective faculties are engaged when we find things beautiful, beauty is not merely relative or dependent on personal taste. Beauty is not only in the "eye of the beholder." Human beings are attracted to universal properties. The properties corral our attention in positive manners. How does this relate to the professions? As professionals, we can embrace and wield these universal aesthetic properties in our work. After all, the eloquent communicator seeks to grab and maintain audience attention in delightful and memorable manners. Aesthetical qualities of presentations, speeches, documents, and even e-mails can spark this attraction.

Through a beauty-minded approach, we can connect objective standards of beauty to modern-day UX or "users experiences." While UX silently consults the rhetorical arts, it also consults the standards of beauty. After all, professional UX designers do not throw together a cluttered website, announce that "beauty is in the eye of the beholder," and then expect a paycheck. Instead, UX designers carefully craft web experiences that may recognize particular cultural trends but also tap into universal standards of beauty that all audiences can get behind.

Let's consult a cognitive law of UX, that is, scientifically proven ways that our brains think about pleasing experiences. An important cognitive law is the aesthetic–usability law of UX, which addresses beauty overall. According to Kate Moran and Kathryn Whitenton from the Nielson Norman Group, users believe that good-looking web designs inevitably work well. In other words, the better a website looks, the more people believe a website is functional. Consequently, UX designers take advantage of this cognitive trend. Although studies support this cognitive phenomenon, experts also caution that the aesthetic–usability law of UX can lead designers astray. Designers can try too hard to be beautiful. And if they are too grand and lush with their aesthetic, they can limit optionality or damage credibility.

Consequently, we should keep moderation in mind. Remember what Cicero tells us about speaking too much in grand style? He says that when speaking too fiery and ornate all the time, people will think us "a raving madman among the sane, like a drunken reveler in the midst of sober men" (*Orator*, Sect. 99). So, for our purposes, we must similarly be careful. We should probably sober our aesthetic. After all, beauty does not solely make something eloquent. But it certainly helps.

Clearly, beautiful things attract attention. People certainly find them delightful to look at. But, as the aesthetic–usability law of UX posits, secondarily, our audiences will also believe that a speech, e-mail, or presentation is more practical if it is good looking. While beauty is certainly persuasive, pretty things do not always work better. Not all good-looking ecommerce websites offer good shopping experiences. Not all good-looking actors are actually good at acting. And all the window dressing in the world cannot save a lousy speech or thoughtless e-mail.

Making Something Beautiful

Influenced by both Plato and Aristotle, Medieval philosopher Thomas Aquinas defines beauty as exhibiting three characteristics: (1) integrity/unity, (2) harmony/proportion, and (3) splendor/radiance (I-I.39.8).

Integrity pertains to the focused wholeness of the composition itself. The internal order generally constructs this sense of unity within our speech or text. Harmony concerns the cooperative proportionate relationships between the internal world of the composition and the external referential world. We can also stretch this definition to include the balanced varied proportions found in the order itself. Finally, splendor involves the radiance of the art: how the art radiates outward, how it captures and awes the public. Therefore, by extension, our speeches and writing can become beautiful if we embrace all three elements: unity, proportionality, and splendor. These characteristics help delight and dazzle our audiences.

Unify

First, let's think about how unity works within something beautiful. People feel secure and hopeful when they encounter something beautiful. Such feelings of warmth can be felt via a composition's internal unity. For instance, the *Mona Lisa* is considered beautiful because of the unity within the composition. The colors, face, hair, eyes, and subtle smile all work toward the oneness of the expression. The parts and dimensions of the painting synchronize to form a holistic cohesion. This cohesion makes people feel good. Another example: An untouched forest tree line at the edge of a plush field might be experienced as beautiful because, again, unity and order pervade the visual experience. By experiencing the tree line, the *beauty in* nature points to the *order of* nature. This natural order is scientifically understood as the order of the universe, which is traced to the Greek word *kosmos*.

Beauty signals an audience's internal understanding of external order. By extension, this understanding of order can blanket people in a warm sense of security. After all, regardless of one's religious, spiritual, or secular beliefs, external order suggests an overarching grand unity that pervades the universe. This reminder about cosmic unity reassures people. As a result, delight washes over them. Are there chaos and bad things happening in the natural world? Of course. But chaos and bad things, such as disease, volcanoes, and wildfires, help moderate the overall balance. Bad stuff serves the grand united order of things. This overall oneness of the *kosmos* delights us because we recognize that naturalness keeps us alive.

This understanding of Nature pervades classical literature: from Homer's *Iliad* and *Odyssey* to Virgil's *Aeneid*. The understanding also pervades classical philosophy's reliance on natural law.

Much like beautiful visual art, compelling musical symphonies, or breathtaking natural vistas, internally organized communication can make readers and listeners feel warm and secure as well. Since unity is a predominant motif of the natural world, eloquent communicators synchronize with their natural inclination to be orderly through unity.

Harmonize

According to the *Oxford English Dictionary*, harmony is "combination of parts or details in accord with each other, so as to produce an aesthetically pleasing effect; agreeable aspect arising from apt arrangement of parts." Therefore, while unity concerns the oneness, harmony concerns the balance of disparate parts. While Aquinas recognizes the balance between the external and the internal harmony, we can consider the proportions within the communication itself.

A piece of art, and by extension, our speaking or writing, should not only rely on unity. Unity can only take us so far. And to be frank, unity can be boring. In contrast, proportionality makes presentations, website, stories, and conversations interesting. Proportionality dynamizes our texts, presentations, or slides. And this dynamism grabs people's attention. After all, would a website grab our attention if it only used soft shades of blue? Would a song interest us if it only used one note? Would a speech excite us if it was robotically spoken without varied inflection? The answer to all of these is, likely, no. Websites grab our attention when they contrast shades of blue with orange. Songs grab our attention when they use a range of notes. Speakers excite us when they vary inflection and volume.

Proportionality celebrates variation, but *balanced, controlled, and purposeful* variation. The unity of our communication tempers the variation in a proportional way so that the variation does not appear or sound chaotic. Proportionality offers difference and contrast, while unity offers sameness and uniformity. Each balances the other. Jesse James Garrett points out in *The Elements of User Experience*, his pivotal book on web

UX, that contrast guides users' eyes toward important parts of the web interface. As such, contrast offer a way to cluster important conceptual groups within the design. In visual design, contrast can be implemented through contrasting colors, light and dark oppositions, bolder fonts, larger fonts, and various other tactics.

Proportional contrast helps audiences follow the message but also delights and persuades audiences. How so? Like unity, proportionality make users feel secure. Order is sexy. Modern science has proven that human beings generally find proportionate and symmetrical faces more attractive than disproportionate and asymmetrical faces. But this revelation is not particularly new. Ancient thinkers, like Pythagoras and Plato, saw mathematics as crucial to understanding the order of the universe. Naturally, they recognized that mathematics fuels music. In late antiquity, Augustine of Hippo recognized that it is order that makes music sound beautiful. Before Augustine, Aristotle expressed a more general insight on order in his *Poetics*. He determined that order acts as a vehicle of beauty itself (1450b34-36). Consequently, proportionate order and unity can make audiences feel good. Therefore, as a dimension of beauty, we can embrace proportionality in our speeches and writing.

As discussed in Chapter 6 on storytelling, people are drawn to dynamic shifts. Change holds our attention. Monotony bores us. Therefore, the difference afforded by aesthetic proportionality engages people. Proportionality invites a dynamism and contrast not only in static images, web design, or prosaic style. Proportionality makes stories or narratives beautiful. Proportionality makes poetry and music beautiful. Proportionality can even make arguments beautiful. While it certainly balances and moderates the composition, proportionality also offers a form of dynamism. When we contrast difference with similarity, we harness a type of energy. We excite our audiences by communicating this energy. And clients and customers will positively associate that dynamic energy with us and our business.

Radiate with Splendor

The third dimension of Aquinas' understanding of beauty, splendor, is the most difficult to grasp. How is splendor fostered? Robert Barron, an

Aquinas scholar who studied in University of Paris (the same university where Aquinas himself taught), explains the Thomistic understanding of splendor with a vivid image. In his 2018 book *The Way of Beauty*, Barron illustrates Aquinas' concept of beauty by referring to early Gothic rose windows found in Medieval churches. These grand round stained-glass windows rotate around a hub with outward spokes forming a perfectly sliced circle.

As the image shows, a rose window can offer a demonstration of Aquinas' theory of aesthetics. After all, Aquinas was influential in the arts. And cathedrals were built with Aquinas' principles in mind. Barron explains that the hub of the Gothic rose window represents the internal unity of beauty, since every spoke is connected fast to the hub. Secondly, proportionality is represented through the equal slices of the circle that extend outward from the hub. But where is evidence of splendor? Barron finally explains that the radiance and splendor is not two dimensional but three-dimensional. The light that shines through the window offers radiance and splendor, the third part of Aquinas' aesthetics. Light shines through the colored glass into the eyes, minds, and hearts of viewers of the window.

Figure 8.1 Rose window at Notre-Dame Cathedral in Paris

Clearly, grand style and figurative language communicates splendor and radiance, even in professional communication. Poetic modes of speaking and writing kindle the heart, not only the head. But what about plain style? Can straightforward professional writing and speaking also radiate splendor? Yes, but it works a bit differently. It radiates splendor in a careful manner, that is, in a manner that is "full of care." Like a cathedral's stained-glass rose window, communicational splendor is indeed three-dimensional: light emanates through the message toward the audience. The author, himself or herself, shines through the composition into the eyes, mind, and heart of the reader. That radiance is care. Our efforts to accommodate audiences are positively noticed. Our readers or listeners recognize the accommodation. This rhetorical care shines into them through the composition or speech as a type of three-dimensional light. Allegorically, our communication can operate similarly to the stained-glass window itself. Compositional cohesion and proportionately help frame the spirit of care so that it appropriately reaches the audience. However, our radiant care, alongside internal order and harmony, kindles feelings of delight in our audience. The integrity, harmony, and radiance become outwardly pleasurable. So, in the Ciceronian manner, our writing or speech delights audiences alongside instructing and persuading them.

For instance, if readers read our lean and orderly e-mails, they may feel a slight surge of delight, even if ever so subtle. Why? From a practical perspective, well-written e-mails evidence that we care for and accommodate our readers. From an aesthetic perspective, our well written e-mails project harmonious order and unity outwardly toward readers. Well-written e-mails radiate respect and accommodation. Although professional e-mails may not radiate splendorous eloquence like the poetry of Ovid, the plays of Shakespeare, or the speeches of Martin Luther King Jr., well-written e-mails offer careful eloquence. That is, they are full of care. This carefulness may not be poetic Splendor (with an uppercase S); however, it offers a rhetorical splendor (with a lowercase s) and manifests radiance.

Beyond Appearances

Ultimately, communication depends on words and language, spoken and written. An effectively flashy visual presentation should act as a means to an end, not as an end itself. Decoration works toward a greater communicative affect. As previously discussed in Chapter 3, communication acts symphonically. Communication should accomplish more than delighting audiences. It should also persuade and teach audiences. If communication were only meant to delight audiences, then communicators would merely spread fun information. In such a world, communicators would primarily seek to make people feel good, and not actually say anything substantive. Socrates cautions against this kind of pleasure-driven rhetoric in the last third of Plato's *Phaedrus*. If communication were only meant for pleasure, communicators would merely tell audiences what audiences want to hear, not truths about situations. Clearly, this pleasure mission introduces the spreading of misinformation. This kind of pleasure-based communication can construct unproductive environments where people neglect answers and ignore best courses of action. It can confuse how human beings understand reality.

It can be argued that priorities of pleasure confuse communication on the Internet these days. Pleasure-driven (rather than truth-driven) communication seems to lead people to embrace misinformation. By seeking pleasure rather than truth, people believe what they want to hear rather than what is actually true. They seek to insulate themselves against uncomfortable truths. And what do we find online? Communities of like-minded individuals who communicate within "echo-chambers." We are probably all familiar with these communities where people speak and write only agreeable stances to one another. Left leaning liberals write only to fellow left-leaning liberal on social media about how being a left-leaning liberal policies are the best. Or right-leaning conservatives may only discuss politics with other right-leaning conservatives on online forums about how right-leaning conservative politics are absolutely right.

Echo-chambers offer pleasurable experiences for participants because like-minded people support one another's positions. They essentially praise one another for being correct. Echo-chambers may make people feel good, but these spaces can be unproductive. Specifically, they isolate people from constructive dialectical interactions. The self-constructed sterility detaches them from fuller understandings of reality.

If we read some Socratic dialogues written by Plato, the solution becomes clear. Classical persuasion and teaching do not seek echo-chambers.

After all, why should persuasion unfold in a community where everyone already believes the same position? Why should teaching unfold in a community where everyone already knows the material? Fruitful communication invites a marketplace of ideas. Therefore, unlike echo-chamber talk, eloquent discourse in the spirit of the classical tradition seeks more than to delight; it also seeks to persuade and instruct diverse audiences.

Accordingly, human experience involves more than sensory pleasures and fleeting emotions. As suggested by philosophers such as Plato and Aristotle, higher order reasoning separates human beings from other animals. Although communication can appeal to our animal appetite to seek "agreeable feelings," eloquent communication strives to transcend superficial inclinations. To this end, professional eloquence seeks to stimulate *intellectual appetites*. In other words, our professional speech and writing should convey arguments, reasoning, and information that connect to our clients, customers, and colleagues. Our intellectual appetites become quenched when we exchange points of view, educate others, and learn from others. In short, style and substance matter when aspiring to be eloquent writers and speakers, much like style and substance matter when aspiring to be an effective readers and listeners. Ideas, words, sentences, and paragraphs matter. Reasoning matters. Knowledge discovery matters. And as Plato acknowledges throughout his corpus: truth-seeking matters. Even in business communication, the heady things still matter.

Beauty and art serve practical purposes. As a form of communication, art can be quite functional. Art can help us better grasp the order of a disorienting, and sometimes chaotic, world. Additionally, beauty can help people better understand abstract concepts such as goodness and truth. In *Phaedrus* and *The Republic*, Plato traces the interrelated triad of transcendentals (beauty, goodness, and truth) in ways that connect us to the unity of Being. This same triad was embraced by Thomas Aquinas and other Christian thinkers hundreds of years after Plato. Since these concepts inform one another, beautiful sensory experiences can point toward higher-level concepts like goodness and truth which sustain our business ethics and professional relationships.

Beauty, as the most sensory accessible in Plato's triad, makes abstract ideas more easily understood. Beauty grabs the attention of our audiences in immediate and positive ways. Consequently, beauty can gracefully escort others into comprehending the other two more cerebral concepts in the triad, goodness and truth. Therefore, if we are looking to lead our audiences and readers toward true and good conclusions about our businesses, products, or services, we may want to first consider the aesthetically pleasing.

Keys to Practical Eloquence

Keep in mind that audiences associate beauty with functionality. Therefore, when audiences encounter beautiful slide decks, writing, and oratory, they associate that with competence.

Unity (oneness), proportionality (variation), and splendor (care for audience) all play important roles in eloquence. Be sure to embrace these characteristics when speaking or writing.

CHAPTER 9

The Eloquent Lifestyle

As discussed in Chapter 1, James Clear's book *Atomic Habits* riffs off Aristotle when highlighting the importance of professional habit building. I am not undercutting the value of Clear's book *Atomic Habits*. It is a valuable book. We should all read it. However, the importance of habits is not new. That said, to be reliably eloquent we should nourish our rhetorical mindsets through routine and repetition. As Clear promotes, when we establish and embrace a new identity, habits will follow. In our case, our new identity is of an eloquent rhetor, speaker, and writer.

Now, part of this identity extends beyond the specific practice of speaking and writing. It also involves the eloquent lifestyle. Such a lifestyle consists of broader workflow habits that supplement our effective communication. The following lifestyle tips offer a series of habits.

Be Social, Be Active

If we stay inside the house by ourselves, we will not elevate our eloquence. And that applies to working from home, as well. The classical tradition probably would not tolerate living through digital screens. After all, screens are not a substitute for real social interaction. Rather, living socially is one is the best ways to develop eloquence. The opportunities are endless. We can go out and speak to friends. Or we can grab coffee with newly hired colleagues who we may not know so well. Or we can strike up conversations in public places with complete strangers.

In these encounters, two types of people will help us grow in eloquence. The first type of person will not be particularly eloquent at all. They may be quiet, scattered, or awkward when they speak. They may stick out as ineffective, or they may merely be "good enough." The second type of person, on the other hand, will be well spoken, focused, and comfortable conversationalists. They will be memorable in a good way. We can learn from both type of people in a dialectical manner. From the first type of person, we can recognize what does not work and avoid it. From the second type of person, we can pick up some good habits. As aspiring eloquent rhetors armed with tips from this book, we should be able to recognize what they do well. How they are clear with their speaking? How do they interest us? How do they engage us? By experiencing what doesn't work and what does work, we should be to apply the observations to our own practices—and accordingly enhance our eloquence.

Ultimately, the world becomes our classroom. And the world can teach us eloquence more fully than only consulting a handbook on eloquence. After all, to repeat Augustine's quotation that we discussed in the Introduction, "... eloquence is picked up more readily by those who read and listen to the words of the eloquent than by those who follow the rules of eloquence" (4.9). As mentioned before, eloquence resembles learning a second or third language, the more we surround ourselves with eloquent people, the more eloquence seeps into our habits of writing and speaking.

Of course, conversing with colleagues and strangers is not the only way to encounter eloquence. We can seek eloquent communicators online. Specifically, we can listen to eloquent podcasts, interviews, or online lectures. The more in-person or virtual time we spend with these eloquent people, the more their eloquence can rub off on us. Motivational speaker Jim Rohm famously notes, "you're the average of the five people you spend the most time with." This point clearly concerns our five most frequent points of contact. But Rohm's point also applies to the podcast hosts that we listen to—and books' authors that we read.

Now, critics of Rohm's "five-person average" often take it too literally. Skeptics argue that Rohm is wrong. For example, what if all of someone's inner circle drink Red Bull? Does that necessarily mean that the individual will drink Red Bull? Obviously not. This literalism takes Rohm's position too specifically. It misses the point. Closer to the spirit of Rohm's "five-person average": we become the average of our inner circle's *priorities*. So, while three of our closest friends may drink Red Bull, they may drink it to be more productive. We may not drink Red Bull like our closest friends, but we may all appreciate the value of productivity. Therefore, our three friends corroborate our priorities in a broader sense.

The same broader influence can apply to eloquence. While we may not parrot the same expressions and inflections as five people from our inner circle, we may adopt similar priorities—good or bad—when speaking or writing. Of course, we don't merely want to choose our friends by their eloquence levels. However, we can still surround ourselves with eloquent influences. We can routinely listen to five eloquent podcasters. We can routinely read the words of five eloquent writers. As such, if we frequently surround ourselves with thinkers who prioritize eloquence, we may start prioritizing similar habits of eloquence. Ultimately, to rephrase Rohm's statement: "We will speak like the average of the five podcasts we most listen to" and "we will write like the average of the five authors we read the most." So, we should thoughtfully choose eloquent podcasters and writers to surround ourselves with.

That said, occasionally, we may adopt specific habits of speech or writing from friends, family members, podcasters, or authors in our lives. If we are adept at mirroring, these explicit imitations may pop up. What is mirroring? According to Vanessa Van Edwards, mirroring is a persuasive tactic that we often do unconsciously. But we can build the habit of conscious mirroring, as well. When we mirror, we imitate our partner's speech patterns or actions. For instance, if they gesture often, we may gesture more. If they use folksy slang, we may also do so. If they regularly share quotations from leadership, we may do so too. As Van Edward points out, studies have proven that mirroring works. Why? It subtly flatters the other person. In other words, the person unknowingly senses that we appreciate what they do and how to speak. And, of course, people typically feel secure in the company of people who resemble themselves. Obviously, mirroring someone else can backfire if our parroting becomes too heavy-handed and deliberate. Ultimately, mirroring should be natural and subtle. And natural mirroring is fostered by habits that we build. And we build those habits by practicing them. So, if we want to get better at mirroring, we should practice mirroring in the world.

Classical rhetorical handbooks (and modern ones, like this one) help guide our trial-and-error practice out in the world. As both Cicero and Augustine tell us, to learn is a necessity. That's what handbooks do. They teach. After understanding how eloquence works, then we can then practice and experiment with moving, motivating, and dazzling others. And recognizing what works and what doesn't work. These second steps require doing. Augustine goes on to explain that we do not—and should not—meticulously consider all rules of eloquence when we speak (4.10). This aligns with Aristotle's definition of rhetoric as the "faculty of observing in any given case the available means of persuasion." Augustine's point: Eloquence is indeed a "faculty" fostered by understanding but it is also nourished by good habits.

Friendship: The Fuel of Eloquence

When teaching a public speaking course at a university years ago, I had a student who was anxious about speaking to large groups of people. In fact, he was virtually paralyzed. Standing up at the front of a 35-student class, he could barely utter a word.

After his first presentation, he met with me after class. He asked if I had any tips that I used when speaking to crowds.

I told him that I never understood the "picture your audience in their underwear" approach. After all, I've never really witnessed large groups of people in their underwear. (Has anyone really?) So how am I supposed to recreate that experience? Instead, I visualize the audience in a more relatable manner: as my own tight-knit friend group. As a result, I adopt a more down-to-earth attitude. And when I do that, the pressure seems to vanish.

During the next class presentation, the student took my advice. He visualized the class as his friend group. And it worked. Sure, he slipped in a few unnecessary curse words into his speech, as he probably would have with his friends, but all in all, he spoke much more smoothly.

It works outside of the public speaking classroom too.

As a professor, I have presented at academic conferences over the years. As you can probably guess, it can be difficult to persuade groups of scholars. Depending on the discipline, they can be stoic, big-headed, or downright combative. So, instead of becoming anxious about my audience, I visualize these scholars as friends rather than strangers or combatants. The results have been favorable. I've connected more with people. I've built stronger professional relationships. The once nerve-racking presentations have become warm conversations.

So how does this work?

It requires much more than fake smiles and honeyed words. For this to work, we need to fire up our imaginations. We need to actually believe that we are among friends when speaking or writing. It may be a charade, but it is a strategic charade.

The approach is pretty basic. Since we care about our friends, we generally talk and write to them with purpose and sincerity. When we visualize *audience members* as friends, the same purposefulness and sincerity radiate effortlessly toward our listeners and readers. They feel this friendly warmth and appreciate it.

When we automatically assume goodwill (as we do in friendship), we naturally assume trust: the bedrock of effective communication. Trust allows ideas to pass more easily between human beings. Trust opens the cognitive flow. Trust keeps us honest. As a result, trustful interactions are much more fluid.

By extension, friendship visualization shields us from our own anxiety. It can safeguard us from suspicious preconceived notions about our audience. Even if the assumptions are true, such suspicion can damage our relationships before they even begin. Its toxic tentacles can wrap around our writing or speaking and choke our confidence. We may begin to fear criticism and doubt ourselves. We may start to walk on eggshells. Our credibility can sputter. Our rapport can fade.

But there is hope. Even if we address groups who seem like unlikeable vultures, we can still address them as friends. And this may even gracefully disarm them in the process. Rather than responding to negativity with more negativity, why not break the vicious circle? Why not assume a position of friendship despite them? Why not think: "Hey, I will treat you as a friend even if you dislike me"? It offers a more caring position. It offers a more confident position.

When we visualize friendship, our speech or writing becomes more humanized. In the 2020 *Harvard Business Review* article "How to Develop Your Leadership Style," Suzanne J. Peterson, Robin Abramson, and R. K. Stutman note a similar advantage. They describe how some leaders (and I would add speakers and writers) communicate with "powerful markers" to strategically announce authority. For example, leaders may use serious inflections, technical jargon, or declarative statements to command the attention of others. Although these markers are useful, they can be overdone. And when overdone, they put people off.

Visualizing friendship helps us avoid relying so much on power displays. Instead, it lends itself to, what the authors label "attractive markers," which project warmth. Similarly, comfortable speaking or writing, as would be natural with our friends, offers a lighter tone, everyday vocabulary, and more conversational questioning and answering. Ultimately, attractive markers temper our power markers, so power markers do not come across as aggressive. As Peterson, Abramson, and Stutman endorse, we can blend both sets of markers. We can moderate powerful style with attractive style to craft "presence" into the writing or speaking. This combination can help connect our audience to our message and build rapport.

Finally, when we visualize friendship, we may also spark reciprocity. That is, we may spark the human tendency to repay kindnesses. As Robert Cialdini notes in *Influence: The Psychology of Persuasion*, human beings are hardwired to reciprocate hospitality. When someone gives us something, we look to repay the favor. The return gift doesn't always need to be proportionate, but receivers feel socially compelled to give back in some way.

Consequently, when we project friendship, audiences often return the favor within the interaction. Audiences may become more engaged in the face-to-face presentation or within a reading experience. That engagement can be their repayment to us. They may also become more friendly in return or be more generous with their attention or time. In short, reciprocity can nudge audiences to participate within the back-and-forth cadence. It energizes dialogue between us and them.

As nineteenth-century German philosopher Friedrich Nietzsche writes in *Human, All Too Human*, "a good writer possesses not only his own spirit but also the spirit of his friends." Effective communication certainly involves "possessing our own spirit" or thinking, but there is more to it than that. Through his dialogues, Plato emphasizes friendly relationships between Socrates and Socrates' dancing partners. After all, friendship and goodwill importantly fuel the "dance of the dialectic" so that the partners do not trip over one another or step on one another's toes.

Eloquence isn't all about us. It concerns our dancing partners as well. Eloquence certainly involves our inward actions (thinking) and outward actions (speaking or writing), but it also involves the inward attitudes of other people. And, as Nietzsche suggests, we can think of those other people as friends. The visualization of friendship reminds us that communication is a social act. It reminds us to celebrate speaking and writing as cooperation and indirectly reminds audiences to do the same.

Friendship building is a habit of eloquence. And Aristotle tells us that we engage in three types of friendship: utility (fleeting friendship based on usefulness), pleasure (also fleeting friendships over shared activities or hobbies), and virtue (enduring friendship over development of character and goodness of one another). Certainly, professional friendships can be utility friendships or pleasurable friendships. However, as eloquent communicators, we should orient ourselves toward the third type of friendship as well. While certainly we help each other get things done and enjoy conversations, we also want to push one another to be better people. When we integrate that third type of friendship into our communication, we will be warmer and more caring. As such, we will be more eloquent.

Write a Lot

In this modern day and age, writing may seem like a "low-tech" option. Why write when we can Snapchat or TikTok? Why write when we can voice-to-text or video call? Writing may require more work. That is true. But that is why writing is so powerful. Although it may seem odd to us in the modern era, the traditional classical perspective leaned into the labor and discipline associated with writing.

According to the wisdom of Crassus quoted by Cicero in *De Oratore*, to be eloquent we should "write as much as possible" because it is "the best and most excellent modeler and teacher of oratory" (1.43). So according to Crassus, the more we write, the better we will be at speaking. How so? He tells us that writing allows us to "examine and contemplate" a subject "in the full light of our intellect" (1.43). And as such, all the ideas and language decisions "must of necessity come under and submit to the keenness of our judgment while writing" (1.43). In other words, we scrutinize grammar, logic, and rhetoric more when we write than when we speak. We have the time and attention to evaluate specific words and ideas with care. These close and careful habits seep into our speech. We more competently and quickly evaluate words and ideas. Crassus even tells us that we can play with arrangement, meter, and rhythm more—and more deeply—when we write. It is difficult to engineer these maneuvers into our speech. But the more we practice them on the page, the more quickly we can deliver them on the "stage."

Yet not all classical thinkers appreciated writing. In *Phaedrus*, Plato's Socrates was suspicious of writing because a written page cannot actively reply to readers like speakers can. He didn't like that writing could not discourse in real time. Moreover, Socrates had another complaint. He argued that we write things down on the page so we don't have to remember them. Therefore, Socrates claimed that our memories would atrophy from writing. And he was right. We see this happening today with the Internet's influence. So much information is stored online or on smartphones that we don't need to remember as much information as we used to.

Despite Plato's objections about the technology of writing, writing remains a useful practice. Specifically, by writing, we organize our thinking. To write down an argument we must consider the reasoning, arrangement of the reasoning, style of the language, and how our audience will possibly receive it. In other words, writing directs our attention to the canons of rhetoric (Chapter 5) much more so than on-the-fly extemporaneous speaking. Believe it or not, it can be useful to spend time writing only to immediately throw the writing in the garbage. Why? The process of writing is valuable. The process is not a waste of time. It helps us learn and understand. The activity of writing organizes our thinking in rich ways. That's why if we want to become an expert on something, we should write a column, an article, or even a book on the subject matter. Writing about something requires deeper understanding than does merely reading a lot about something. While reading offers us input, writing requires input, analyzing and synthesizing that input with other input, and then finally rhetorically composing *output*. In short, writing requires more activity from our brains. And it requires thoughtful consideration of the communication with other people.

We should remember that not everything has to be a product. Eloquent men and women embrace strong processes, not only products. And writing helps us deeply dive into these composition processes.

Writing helps us distill our thinking through various actions, such as the mechanical task of typing words, the mental task of choosing words and arrangements, and the task of rereading our own writing as we rhetorically refine it for audiences.

In sum, the writing process helps us understand. In Letter 143 of his personal correspondence, Augustine tells us that he wrote to progress and progressed to write. As professionals, we should remember Augustine's symbiotic relationship. Writing helps us move forward as eloquent thinkers and communicators. At the same time, innovative thinking requires that we refine our ideas through the act of writing and eloquently share them with others through written texts.

Read a Lot

Reading is another fruitful "low-tech" activity that we can reconsider. If we really think about how to effectively read, and if we think about reading to get the most out of our time, we may recognize that reading is far from a simple process. It demands more than gobbling words, sentences, and paragraphs with our eyes. It involves stopping and starting. It involves rereading, reflection, note-taking, and even skipping parts of books. When we read, we employ purposeful habits, both mental and physical, as we digest wisdom from an article or book.

In today's "high-tech" world, we often resort to TED talks, podcasts, and audiobooks to streamline our learning. Clearly, these resources help us squeeze education into our hectic lives. This can be wonderful. However, we shouldn't overlook the art of reading. Reading has some serious advantages built into it. We can sometimes forget these advantages when dazzled by the newest conveniences and the fastest technologies. Ultimately, reading can help us propel our learning in ways that podcasts and TED talks cannot.

Clearly, reading takes more time than listening to a podcast or an abridged audiobook. In the modern fast-paced world, it may seem disadvantageous to spend long periods of time doing anything. After all, why read a book for an hour every day for a month when we can listen to a podcast for 20 minutes a week? And why read a book throughout 2 months when we can listen to an audiobook in 7 hours?

Podcasts, audiobooks, and TED talks may expose us to new concepts at a faster pace, and this seems great though it is not without its dangers. These technologies can prompt some important questions: Does "quicker" learning necessarily mean "better" learning? Are we sacrificing the *quality* of material for the *quantity* of material? Are we truly internalizing and applying the wisdom from TED talks? Or are we hastily consuming data that we will soon forget?

Reading books can increase the odds of actually remembering what we learn and applying that learned material. After all, reading takes more time, allowing us to absorb the ideas more patiently. Since reading often unfolds over days and weeks, writers' ideas percolate in our minds for longer. We steep in their concepts, point-of-view, and arguments for longer. We can internalize them for longer, live with them for longer, and apply them to the world around us for longer—which can ultimately help us more effectively grow from that knowledge.

As Robert Greene outlines throughout his 2013 book *Mastery*, mastering a subject takes strategy and time. Learning does not happen through osmosis. It takes work. This point may seem obvious, but it's often overlooked. The experience of reading can ensure that we are patient with our time as we learn. Patience may be a difficult pill to swallow in today's quickly moving world, but it acts as a key educational ingredient that is naturally cultivated when reading.

We may also forget that reading books offers a very different experience from listening to a podcast or watching a TED talk. Unlike spoken and visual media, reading intimately places us inside the mind of an author, presumably, an expert author. The words on the page transport us into an expert's knowledgeable headspace.

Since reading requires intimate time with ideas, the ideas can spend more intimate time *with us*. As a result, we remember concepts more fully, and we remember the author more fully, after spending such intimate time with them. The ideas stick to our bones with more staying power. Therefore, if we really want to emulate particularly successful individuals and learn what they know, we may want to visit their books to really crawl inside their heads.

Furthermore, we have more control over our learning experience when we read. Think about this the next time you read an article or book.

Do you notice how you actively control your movement through the text when you read? Inevitably, we control our own experience to get what we want from the text. This control can be advantageous. Unlike podcasts and TED talks, reading can proceed in our own time. We are not necessarily at the mercy of a speaker or a presenter. We do not have to follow their pace, even when we toggle through the limited number of reading speeds found on digital platforms. Instead, we can put down the book, think, reread a paragraph, and flip back to a previous section, all before moving forward again. Technically, we can do this when we listen to a podcast or watch a TED talk, that is, we can rewind, pause, or rewatch, but we often don't.

Books encourage us to patiently move through ideas on the page. This movement unfolds mentally but also physically. As such, we can physically make the text our own. We may want to underline passages, write blurbs in the margins, or dog-ear interesting pages. This active physical activity mirrors our active mental activity. Moreover, it makes it easier to revisit and reread the text in the future. In short, reading books give us the option to physically interact and make a text our own. Podcasts and TED talks rarely afford us these material luxuries.

Learning through podcasts, TED talks, and audiobooks is certainly better than not learning at all. We certainly want to seize all opportunities to feed our appetite for professional growth. However, we can feed it strategically. If we are serious about developing ourselves as professionals, we should think about diversifying our learning. In other words, it does not have to be a zero-sum game. Rather than *substituting* our reading practices with visual and spoken media, we can *supplement* our reading practices with digital media. If we push ourselves to prioritize reading and complement reading with newer media approaches, we will elevate the quality of our learning. We will notice a clear improvement in our professional performance—and others will notice it as well.

Now that this *Influence with Eloquence* reading journey has ended, you can consult the appendix for a reading list so that you can embark on future journeys to refine your eloquence. Eloquence is not something established overnight. It takes incremental changes throughout our lives. If we keep exposing ourselves to eloquent speakers and writers, and if we keep practicing the strategies and tactics of classical eloquence, eventually there will come a point when we'll genuinely wow ourselves. After writing a proposal or delivering a pitch, we will notice the persuasive impact it has had on our audience. They will nod to our message, wear smiles on their faces, and be moved to act. In those moments, we recognize, "Hey, I was pretty eloquent!" But we can't stop there. If we hone our craft, these satisfying moments will become more frequent. And so will our success.

Bibliography

Anderson, Chris. *TED Talks: The Official TED Guide to Public Speaking*. Mariner, 2016.

Aquinas, Thomas. *The Summa Theologica (Vols. 1–4)*. Translated by Fathers of the English Dominican Province. Benziger Brothers, 1948.

Aquinas, Thomas. *Commentaries on Aristotle's "On Sense and What Is Sensed" and "On Memory and Recollection."* Translated by Kevin White. Catholic University of America Press, 2005.

Aristotle. *On the Soul; Parva Naturalia; On Breath*. Translated by W. S. Hett. Harvard University Press, 1957.

Aristotle. *Metaphysics*. Translated by Hugh Tredennick. Harvard University Press, 1980.

Aristotle. *Poetics*. Translated by Stephen Halliwell. Harvard University Press, 1995.

Aristotle. *Nicomachean Ethics*. Translated by Terence Irwin. Hackett, 1999.

Aristotle. *Rhetoric*. Translated by W. Rhys Roberts. Dover, 2004.

Atwill, Janet M. *Rhetoric Reclaimed: Aristotle and the Liberal Arts Tradition*. Cornell University Press, 1998.

Augustine. *On Instructing the Unlearned; Concerning Faith of Things not Seen; On the Advantage of Believing; The Enchiridion to Laurentius, or, Concerning Faith, Hope, and Charity*. Parker and Co., 1885.

Augustine. *The Immortality of the Soul, the Magnitude of the Soul, On Music, The Advantage of Believing, on Faith in Things Unseen*. Catholic University of America Press, 2002.

Augustine. *On Christian Teaching*. Translated by R. P. H. Green. Oxford University Press, 2008.

Barron, Robert. *The Way of Beauty*. Word on Fire, 2018.

Berkshire Hathaway. "Shareholder Letters." Accessed November 29, 2024. https://berkshirehathaway.com/letters/letters.html.

Bezos, Jeff. "2016 Letter to Shareholders." *Amazon*, April 17, 2017. https://aboutamazon.com/news/company-news/2016-letter-to-shareholders.

Saint Bonaventure. *On the Reduction of the Arts to Theology*. Translated by Zachary Hayes. Franciscan Institute Publications, 1996.

Brandenburger, Adam M., and Barry J. Nalebuff. *Co-opetition*. Doubleday, 1998.

Brown, Laura. *The Only Business Writing Book You Ever Need*. W.W. Norton, 2019.

Cabane, Olivia Fox. *The Charisma Myth*. Portfolio, 2012.

Chesterton, G. K. *Orthodoxy*. Sam Torode Book Arts, 2008. Originally published 1908.

Cialdini, Robert B. *Influence: The Psychology of Persuasion*. First Harper Business, 2021.

Cicero, Marcus Tullius. *De Oratore*. Translated by J. S. Harper. Harper & Brothers, 1860.

Cicero, Marcus Tullius. *De Inventione; De Optimo Genere Oratorum; Topica*. Translated by H. M. Hubbell. Harvard University Press, 1949.

Cicero, Marcus Tullius. *Rhetorica ad Herennium*. Translated by Henry Caplan. Harvard University Press, 1954.

Cicero, Marcus Tullius. *Orator*. Translated by H. M. Hubbell. Harvard University Press, 1971.

Clear, James. *Atomic Habits*. Penguin, 2018.

Dalio, Ray. *Principles*. Simon & Schuster, 2017.

Demetrius. *A Greek Critic: Demetrius on Style*. Translated by G. M. A. Grube. University of Toronto Press, 1961.

Dixit, Avinash K., and Barry J. Nalebuff. *The Art of Strategy: A Game Theorist's Guide to Success in Business and Life*. W.W. Norton, 2010.

Dweck, Carol. *Mindset: The New Psychology of Success*. Ballantine, 2007.

Epstein, David J. Range. Penguin, 2021.

Fisher, Roger, William Ury, and Bruce Patton. *Getting to Yes: Negotiating Agreement without Giving In*. Penguin, 2011.

Gallagher, David M. "Thomas Aquinas on Self-Love as the Basis for Love of Others." *Acta Philosophica* 8 (1999): 23–44.

Gallo, Carmine. "The Art of Persuasion Hasn't Changed in 2,000 Years." *Harvard Business Review*, July 2019. https://hbr.org/2019/07/the-art-of-persuasion-hasnt-changed-in-2000-years.

Gallo, Carmine. *The Presentation Secrets of Steve Jobs*. McGraw-Hill, 2016.

Gallo, Carmine. *The Bezos Blueprint*. St. Martins, 2022.

Garrett, Jesse James. *The Elements of User Experience*. New Riders, 2003.

Godin, Seth. *All Marketers are Liars*. Penguin, 2009.

Gorgias. "Gorgias' Encomium of Helen." Translated by George Kennedy. In *The Older Sophists*. Edited by Rosamond Kent Sprague. Hackett, 2001.

Greene, Robert. *The 33 Strategies of War*. Penguin, 2007.

Greene, Robert. *Mastery*. Penguin, 2013.

Hagel III, John. "Every Company Needs a Narrative." *Harvard Business Review*, May 25, 2021. https://hbr.org/2021/05/every-company-needs-a-narrative.

Horace. *Horace, Satires and Epistles; Persius, Satires*. Translated by Niall Rudd. Penguin, 2005.

Hugh of St. Victor. *Didascalicon*. Translated by Jerome Taylor. Columbia University Press, 1991.

"iPhone 1—Steve Jobs MacWorld Keynote in 2007—Full Presentation, 80 mins." Posted May 17, 2013, YouTube. Accessed December 4, 2024. https://youtube.com/watch?v=VQKMoT-6XSg.

"Jeff Bezos: The Amazon Origin Story—Groundbreaking 2001 Interview." YouTube. Accessed December 12, 2024. https://youtube.com/watch?v=KkIiPyqxock.

John of Salisbury. *Metalogicon*. Translated by Daniel D. McGarry. Paul Dry, 2019.

Joseph, Miriam. *The Trivium in College Composition and Reading*. Martino, 2014. Reprint of 1948 (3rd ed.).

Kahneman, Daniel. *Thinking Fast and Slow*. Farrar, Straus and Giroux, 2013.

Krug, Steve. *Don't Make Me Think!* New Riders, 2013.

Lanham, Richard. *The Economics of Attention: Style and Substance in the Age of Information*. University of Chicago Press, 2007.

Lents, Nathan H. "Why Are Symmetrical Faces So Attractive?" *Psychology Today*, July 8, 2019. https://psychologytoday.com/us/blog/beastly-behavior/201907/why-are-symmetrical-faces-so-attractive.

Longinus. *On Great Writing*. Translated by G. M. A. Grube. Hackett, 1991.

MacRae, Paul. *Business and Professional Writing: A Basic Guide for Americans*. Broadview Press, 2016.

May, Matthew E. *The Laws of Subtraction*. McGraw-Hill, 2013.

McCormack, Mark H. *What They Don't Teach You at Harvard Business School*. Bantam, 1986. Originally published 1984.

McKee, Robert. *Dialogue: The Art of Verbal Action for Page, Stage, and Screen*. Twelve, 2016.

McKee, Robert, and Thomas Gerace. *Storynomics: Story-Driven Marketing in the Post-Advertising World*. Twelve, 2018.

McKeon, Richard. "Rhetoric and Poetic in Aristotle." In *Aristotle's Poetics and English Literature*, edited by Elder Olson. University of Chicago Press, 1965.

Meadows, Richard. *Optionality: How to Survive and Thrive in a Volatile World*. Thales Press, 2020. Kindle edition.

Moran, Kate. "The Aesthetic-Usability Effect." *Neilson Normal Group*. February 3, 2024. https://nngroup.com/articles/aesthetic-usability-effect/.

Munter, Mary, and Lynn Hamilton. *Guide to Managerial Communication*. 10th ed. Pearson, 2013.

O'Toole, James, and Warren G. Bennis. "A Culture of Candor." *Harvard Business Review*, June 2009, 54–61.

Perelman, Chaim, and Lucie Olbrechts-Tyteca. *The New Rhetoric: A Treatise on Argumentation*. Translated by John Wilkinson and Purcell Weaver. 1969. University of Notre Dame Press, 2010.

Peterson, Suzanne J., Robin Abramson, and R. K. Stutman. "How to Develop Your Leadership Style." *Harvard Business Review*, November–December 2020, 69–77.

Pink, Daniel H. *To Sell Is Human*. Canongate, 2013.

Plato. *Gorgias*. Translated by Donald J. Zeyl. Hackett, 1987.

Plato. *Crito*. In *Five Dialogues*. Translated by G. M. A. Grube, Hackett, 2002, 45–57.

Plato. *Phaedrus*. Translated by Stephen Scully. Hackett, 2003.

Quintilian. *Institutes of Oratory*. Translated by John Shelby Watson. 1856. Revised and edited by Lee Honeycutt and Curtis Dozier. Createspace, 2015.

Robertson, Donald. "Introduction." In Seneca, *Letters from a Stoic*. Translated by Richard Mott Gummere. Capstone, 2021.

Rumelt, Richard. *Good Strategy, Bad Strategy: The Difference and Why It Matters*. Profile Books, 2017.

Scott, Kim. *Radical Candor: Be a Kick-Ass Boss Without Losing Your Humanity*. St. Martin, 2017.

Sextus Empiricus. *Against Professors*. Translated by R. G. Bury. Harvard University Press, 1949.

Sinek, Simon. *Start with Why*. Portfolio, 2011.

Stull, Edward. *UX Fundamentals for Non-UX Professionals*. Apress, 2018.

Sullivan, Jay. *Simply Said*. Wiley, 2016.

Taleb, Nassim Nicholas. *The Bed of Procrustes*. Random House, 2016.

Taylor, Charles. *A Secular Age*. Harvard University Press, 2007.

Tubis, Nick. "First Principles Thinking: The Blueprint for Solving Business Problems." *Forbes Magazine*, September 13, 2023.

Van Edwards, Vanessa. *Cues*. Portfolio, 2022.

Van Edwards, Vanessa. "How to Sell Any Idea in 7 Effective Steps." *Science of People*, November 7, 2024. https://scienceofpeople.com/sell-an-idea/.

Whitenton, Katheryn. "The Aesthetic Usability Effect and Prioritizing Appearance vs. Functionality." *Neilson Normal Group*, 2024. https://nngroup.com/videos/aesthetic-usability-effect/.

Wong, Euphemia. "Serial Position Effect: How to Create Better User Interfaces." *Interaction Design Foundation*, 2020. https://interaction-design.org/literature/article/serial-position-effect-how-to-create-better-user-interfaces.

Zak, Paul A. "Neuroscience of Trust: Management Behaviors that Foster Employee Engagement." *Harvard Business Review*, January–February, 2017, 84–90.

APPENDIX 1

Further Readings

Top ten practical classical works on eloquence/rhetoric/story. Ranked for priority.

1. Aristotle's *Rhetoric*
2. Cicero's *De Oratore*
3. Aristotle's *Poetics*
4. Plato's *Gorgias*
5. Demetrius' *On Style*
6. Horace's *Ars Poetica*
7. Quintilian's *Institutio Oratoria*
8. Augustine's *De Doctrina Christina* (Book Four)
9. Isocrates' *Against the Sophists*
10. Longinus' *On Great Writing*

Top ten contemporary handbooks on eloquence/rhetoric/story informed by the classical tradition. Ranked for priority.

1. Mortimer Adler's *How to Speak, How to Listen* (1983/1997)
2. Ward Farnsworth's *The Socratic Method: A Practitioner's Handbook* (2021)
3. Robert McKee's *Story* (1997)
4. Jack Hart's *Wordcraft* (2021)
5. Peter Boghossian and James Lindsay's *How to Have Impossible Conversations* (2019)
6. Mortimer Adler's *How to Read a Book* (1940/1970)
7. Miriam Joseph's *The Trivium in College Composition and Reading* (Third Ed.) (1948)
8. Robert Greene's *The Art of Seduction* (2001)
9. Robert McKee's *Dialogue* (2016)
10. Jack Hart's *Storycraft* (2011)

APPENDIX 2

Glossary

Aesthetics—The study of beauty.

Confirmatio (Confirmation)—The middle part of a classical speech where the positive proof is presented.

Dialectic—"Cooperative competition" or the back-and-forth exchange of perspectives "across" two parties in pursuit of truth.

Dignitas—The virtue of respecting the dignity of people, especially when escorting them toward excellence.

Enthymeme—A logical syllogism without a communicated premise. Sometimes referred to as a rhetorical syllogism.

Ethos (appeal to)—Rhetorically emphasizing the character or trustworthiness of the speaker or writer within a composition.

Eudaimonia—Living a good life and pursuing excellence for its own sake.

Exordium—The beginning or "hook" of a classical speech that places the audience in the appropriate frame of mind.

Grammar—The art of translating experience and references into symbols that can be communicated.

Gravitas—The virtue of taking topics seriously, specifically ones that deserve to be taken seriously.

Hypomonē—Patiently continuing toward life goals despite the obstacles.

Kairos—The opportune moment to speak or write.

Kosmos—Naturally ordered harmony of the universe.

Logic—The art of thinking, or processing ideas, about reality.

Logos (appeal to)—Within speech or piece of writing, rhetorically drawing attention to the logic, argument, or dimensions of reality.

Makrothumia—A form of patience that means "slow to anger." Not allowing oneself to immediately become upset by other people.

Momento mori—Meditating upon one's own moment of death to help bring perspective.

Narratio (Narration)—The second part of a classical speech which states facts or background so that the audience knows about the circumstances before the formal argument is presented.

Officia oratoris—The offices of the orator or rhetor: to teach, to delight, and to move.

Partitio—This brief section of a classical speech outlines of the structure of a speaker's argument. It is stated toward the beginning of a speech. Also called the *divisio*.

Pathos (appeal to)—Rhetorically evoking emotion from the audience within a composition.

Peroratio (Conclusion)—The conclusion of a classical speech which often appeals to pathos and summarizes the argument.

Phronesis—Practical wisdom.

Poetics—While poetry is a part of classical poetics, poetics subsumes the art of storytelling in its wider sense, including narrative plot, characters, and spectacle.

Praxis—Action informed by theory.

Premise—A proposition that acts as a foundation of an argument or inference. It is often one of the two propositions of a syllogism.

Proposito—This short section of a speech announces the main position of a speaker's argument. It is traditionally stated toward the beginning of a classical speech.

Refutatio (Refutation)—Often placed toward the end of a classical speech, this section of a speech provides negative proofs or objections to the argument. The section also replies to these counterarguments.

Rhetoric—The art of effective or influential communication. Aristotle defines rhetoric as "the faculty of observing the available means of persuasion."

Syllogism—A transparently deductive logical structure with communicated premises and conclusion.

Telos—An ultimate goal or end.

Trivium—Trifold cooperation of grammar, logic, and rhetoric that is central to effective communication. The foundations of the classical liberal arts.

About the Author

Gavin F. Hurley, PhD, is an associate professor of communication and literature at Ave Maria University where he teaches rhetoric, writing, and business communication at both under-graduate and graduate levels. His scholarship on rhetoric has appeared in academic journals such as *Journal for the History of Rhetoric*, *Journal of Communication and Religion*, and *Philosophy of Management*. Over the years, he has published over a dozen essays on the rhetoric of film and literature for essay collections. His book *Catholic Horror and Rhetorical Dialectics* was published by Lehigh University Press in 2024.

Dr. Hurley can be found at https://gavinfhurley.com.

Index

www.ingramcontent.com/pod-product-compliance
Lightning Source LLC
Chambersburg PA
CBHW061307220326
41599CB00026B/4772